D0881169

A DRIVING PASSION

A DRIVING
PASSION

By Marco Vassi

Preface by Norman Mailer

THE PERMANENT PRESS
Sag Harbor, NY 11963

Copyright © 1992 by The Permanent Press

All rights reserved, including the right to reproduce this book, or parts thereof, in any form, except for the inclusion of brief quotations in a review.

Library of Congress Cataloging-in-Publication Data

Vassi, Marco.
    A driving passion / by Marco Vassi ; with a preface by Norman Mailer.
        p.   cm.
    ISBN 1-877946-19-2 : $21.95
    1. Erotic literature, American.   I. Title.
PS3572.A86D75   1992
814'.54—dc20

                                                    91-40181
                                                    CIP

Manufactured in the United States of America

THE PERMANENT PRESS
Noyac Road
Sag Harbor, NY 11963

EDITOR'S NOTE

In the spring of 1975, at the height of the "sexual revolution," Marco Vassi gave a series of lectures on eroticism at Anthos, a human potential center in New York City. *A Driving Passion* is the edited transformation of those tape-recorded sessions.

As he voyaged into the worlds of heterosexuality, homosexuality, perversions, marriage, and fidelity, he detailed his observations with the baseness of Rabelais, the ecstasy of Ram Dass, the raunchiness of Henry Miller, and the humor of Lenny Bruce.

At the time of his death in January, 1989, he was generally considered to be the world's pre-eminent erotic novelist, his books being published in the United States, the United Kingdom, Japan, Spain, Germany, Portugal, and Scandinavia. It is my hope that *A Driving Passion* will provide an even more intimate glimpse of the man himself and the forces that drove him.

Martin Shepard

CONTENTS

PREFACE

by Norman Mailer

To entertain a large generalization, I would say
there are two kinds of philosophers: those who build
their structure upon the work of other philosophers
as opposed to what I would call pioneers—that is,
writers who develop their philosophy from the jour-
neys of their life. This second category (one thinks of
Rousseau and Nietzsche) does not owe that much to
what has gone before.

Marco Vassi was a philosopher of the second vari-
ety. He was by any average standard a minor writer,
which is to say that he never succeeded in getting his
whole view of life into at least one truly important
book. His concerns, however, were major, and he
went far with them—often by way of his extraordinary magazine essays. His theme was Metasex. He

9

coined the word to stand for all the varieties of sex that explore to the side, beneath, or beyond the act of procreation. Procreation was sex, but any other use of the act was Metasex, and Vassi believed (if he never put it exactly this way) that in Metasex were the secrets of individual health and the good society. One could not find oneself (that is, acquire the healing secret) unless one explored to the end of one's sexual inclinations. Even for the late fifties and sixties, Vassi carried it pretty far. He went way beyond the threesomes, foursomes and more gala endeavors of the orgy. As a presumptive heterosexual, he also voyaged past bondage and domination into personal degradation. He uses the concept of degradation—it is his word— to describe being corn-holed by a dozen men in a Turkish bath; in short, he did everything. He was a philosopher, with that notebook of the mind that speaks of immaculate detachment. He got into about every kind of sexual, that is, Metasexual, relation possible with men and women, he even got married.

He was a sexual explorer, but he was born and raised a Catholic. If Catholicism has many faces, its presence in the psyche of a sexual explorer must be felt first as a great weight. Marco Vassi was a mountain climber who carried this impost in his psychic knapsack, and what it must have cost him is hard to measure. I met him only once for a brief period, long enough to shake hands and say hello, but he looked small and tired. He was hardly as imposing as that intrepid and incredibly honest navigator who recounted his sexual adventures in a strong clear literary style capable of handling all the paradoxes of his exceptional experiences. Of course, one of the marks of good writers is that they should not in person be as handsome as their works—it is better when the best of themselves goes into their writing. Besides, he may have been ill. I met him only two or three years before he died. Perhaps the HIV virus had entered him already.

In any event, he died of AIDS without putting up any great fight. It is not surprising. He was a serious philosopher and the mark of the species is to live and die by one's ideas. He saw Metasex as the healing agent. The world was dying for lack of communication among all of us humans, and sex was not only there for procreation, but in its larger form, as Metasex, was there to accelerate communication. I expect he believed that no faster way existed to speed up a relationship than by way of Metasex. Humans would cross the abyss between themselves and others by entering the playgrounds and jungles of sex.

It was his philosophy, and he articulated it and explored its moral ramifications in a dozen works, all interesting. At his best, which was surprisingly often considering the inroads on his energy, he wrote beautifully, but then he was writing on the wave of his philosophy which was that Metasex would give him all the energy he needed.

I think it was for this reason that he put up no fight against his terminal disease. He had put all his bets on one hypothesis—exactly the impulse of an ambitious philosopher—and when he lost (for he had to see his disease as a refutation of what he believed) there was much less point in continuing to live. Philosophers are the first of the species to die of a broken heart and Marco Vassi proves the case. He was his own experiment, and, ipso facto, a rare mortal. There are not that many men and women who come out of a religious background who are willing to spend their lives trying to stare into God's eyes, knowing all the while that if they are forced to blink, they must accept the full significance.

Let me leave you with *A Driving Passion*. It is, in effect, an introduction and overview of all his other books, and my hope is that it will lead readers to explore the bold literary contribution of Marco Vassi.

BACKGROUNDS

1. A DRIVING PASSION

JACK DANIELS . . .

Eroticism is a real pleasure in life. But it can be a disease, a distraction, a habit, just like anything else. I work at *Penthouse*. We recently hired a twenty-six-year-old guy as an editor. He came from someplace in Missouri, was in a new city, walked in and all he could see were the asses of the one hundred women who work there. He's typing and working, but if you look in his eyes and you talk to him you see that he's responding on one level while you can see ass all over his face.

I see it too, and I'm thirty-seven. The guy I work for sees it and he's sixty-five. We all sit around and we all have to deal with it in our various ways and from our various levels of experience and age. Yet why should it be such a compulsion—such an overwhelming obsession? None of us is really horny. Nobody has any real trouble getting laid. You can come as often as you need to. I don't think there are too many people with really serious dysfunctional problems like, "I can't come. I can't get it up. It doesn't get wet. It doesn't go down." We can all pretty well do it. So why does it grab us in that way?

Let's put it this way. Everybody's looking for the same thing. Everybody wants to feel good. Everybody wants to be happy, to put it in the baldest terms. I think, for most of us, given where we live in time and space, that usually translates into a form of relaxation. We're all looking to break through the tensions of all the movements we endure and relax. We want to feel good, we want to feel a flow, we want to feel like it's happening with us. Balling is obviously one of our prime tools for doing this. Nothing will cool you out and straighten you out and make you feel good like a good fuck. A really good fuck and it's "Ah, Jesus. That really feels good. What was I so uptight about? What was I so crazy about?"

It seems that pleasure comes from that kind of relaxation. That release of tension has been built into us in order that we will do a peculiar thing; that I will go over to that creature and stick part of me into part of it. Very absurd behavior. Why would I want to do that? Because of all that it feels. The feeling is there so that we will engage in the biological purpose. But we have learned that we can do that without having to fulfill its primary purpose. Because we want that FEEL-GOOD—that sense of opening and relaxing—we are driven, psychologically, to repeat and repeat and repeat this act.

We all go through loops. We all go through two days or two weeks or two months where it couldn't interest us less. And then, Zap! You can see people drooling when it suddenly comes on them. I think that happens to females as well as males, where sometimes it's lip licking time and "I've just got to have it."

It's hard to remember a time when Metasexuality hasn't been the essence of my lifestyle. It's been a driving passion. One lady commented that as an artist, she can feel energy through walking down the street or through her painting. That's true for me too. I can get high in many many ways. But Metasex is my Jack Daniels. It's always there at my side. I'll take a little of your drink or toke a little of your grass and all, but I've got my Jack Daniels with me. That's the one I know best. It's my special gift and curse.

METASEX. . .

Q: You use the word Metasex rather than Sex to describe your erotic adventures. Why?

M: Metasex is a word that I coined after coming upon the realization that Sex is what you do to make babies. That biological equivalent has been given us for the same reason that it's been given just about every other life form on the planet, which is to perpetuate itself. Now what godly or ungodly reason nature has for wanting us to perpetuate ourselves, I haven't the foggiest idea. But that seems to be our purpose. Somebody puts us here, we come along, we start somebody else off, we pass on, and they seem to continue what it is that's happening. It's a very mysterious business. Why we are here, why we perpetuate ourselves, what it means to give birth and what it means to die are matters shrouded in mystery and unknowing, except for those who are fortunate enough to have some kind of mythic structure to believe in which explains the entire thing.

So Sex is all that. It is a very very serious organic, biological and moral involvement. When you mate and you have a child you immediately plunge yourself into questions of mortality, continuation of the species, how the civilization is to be run, since I have a child what kind of world am I bringing it into, and how am I contributing to the kind of world that it is.

Most of what I do in bed or out of bed has nothing

to do with all that. Whether I do it with a woman, or a man, or a man and a woman, whether it's romantic or whether it's sado-masochistic, whether we're doing water games in the bathroom—all of that has nothing to do with these very weighty questions which Sex seems to imply. It uses the same organs and it uses the same energy but it's something else, for we do it for other reasons. There are all kinds of motivations for indulging this erotic activity aside from making a baby. I thought, "If it's something different, it needs a different name." So I called it Metasex—as in Meta-physics—that which is beyond Sex.

When I got to thinking, "What is Metasex?" I began to look at myself. What is it that I do? Then I began looking around at other people. I found that in any given group of individuals, you're going to find some-body who likes to whip, somebody who likes to be whipped, guys who like guys, women who like women and men, people who like animals, people who like to get pissed on in the shower (water sports), people who like to be degraded.

Since my particular mode of life is to first look at things subjectively, I realized that I do all these things. Then I talked to all the people I did these things with, and I found that everybody does everything and it's all right. Now if you start thinking about this in rela-tion to Sexual criteria, you're going to get hung up. According to Sexual criteria, homosexuality is ob-viously a perversion, no question about it. It has nothing to do with making a baby. It's perverse. Les-bianism is perverse. Bisexuality is perverse. Orgies

are perverse. Contraception is perverse. Just about
everything that we do according to Sexual criteria is
perverse. It occurred to me that a lot of the hangups
that we have—aside from the simple problems of
"How do I get laid?" or, "I'm getting laid too much.
How do I stop getting laid," or, "I got married in
order to get laid and now my old lady or my old man
won't give me any, so I got rid of my old lady or my
old man but nobody in the bars will talk to me"—aside
from these realistic problems, the psychological problems arise from constantly thinking of Metasexual
behavior in terms of Sexual criteria. You're a guy and
you like to suck a cock. You wonder, "Is there something wrong with this?" Sexually, yes. But it would be
just as wrong if a woman did it.

I was raised as a Catholic and rebelled and ran away
and did all the things that we all do with our childhood religious trips. But the hipper I got, the more I
found myself sounding like a Catholic. It was weird. I
was getting so far out, yet I was saying things like, "Of
course, from a Sexual viewpoint, contraception is
wrong." I thought, "Can it be? After all my
pyrotechnics, to wind up back in the arms of Mother
Church?" Well, Sexually, yes. Mother Church was
right. There she is, in her wisdom, saying "If you
accept Sex is for this purpose, and if you do it for any
other reason, including pleasure, it's wrong." The
splendor and the pain and all the rest of it is Metasex.
And this is what most of us do 99 percent of the time.

Metasex is something we are more familiar with
than Sex itself. Sometimes it has to do with the seek-

ing of pain. Sometimes it has to do with the seeking of knowledge. It can be hedonistic but is not necessarily so. In Tantric Yoga, not only do you experience pleasure, but if you become aware of the physical aspects of what you're doing, you've blown it, since in Tantra, Metasex is utilized to transcend the physical.

Implicit in Metasex is the concept that if you're not fucking to make a baby, why put labels on it? If you're getting fucked in the ass or you're in a threesome or getting whipped or necking on the couch, it doesn't matter. It's all Eros; the God Eros descending and putting us into that space which we all know about. If you're not making a baby, there is no qualitative difference between what two men do together and what a man and a woman do together. It's a different psychological experience. You can play different games and use different muscles, but in terms of a Metasexual experience, you feel the same kinds of things: the same sensations, the same feelings of love, hatred, excitement, and orgasms.

Metasexuality is a useful term because it helps end these artificial divisions between people. It's a funny thing that happens with liberation movements. The same thing is happening in the erotic realm as happened in the political realm; the more everybody shouts "Unity," the more splinter groups there are. So the Lesbians meet. The Eulenspiegel Society (sadomasochists) meets. The Gay men meet. The Bisexuals meet. The Singles meet. The Recently Divorced meet. And what does that mean? If you're recently divorced do you only want to fuck somebody that's recently divorced? You know what's going to happen. You're going to talk about your marriages, get sentimental, and you're going to wind up getting married again.

God has an infinity of faces. That particular God, Eros, just keeps coming down all the time. There's a hundred times a day when you look at people and sort of fuck them; not just looking at asses or looking at eyes. But you meet somebody and a murmur comes to your lips. That little shimmer comes down. Sometimes it's not a mutual thing. Sometimes it is. But when it comes down it's akin to Grace. "Oh God, that feels good." The question is, "What do you do with it?" That's what everybody's really interested in. The only thing I have to say about it is find out who you are, find out what you want, and if you have the courage, live that.

One of the most difficult things is to really feel and really go with what you want. Because you've got all kinds of voices inside you and voices outside of you telling you all sorts of things.

First they tell you "it's wrong to be gay. It's sick." Then they tell you, "If you're not gay you're sick." It used to be if you were a guy and you enjoyed sucking cocks, "Wow. Nothing worse." Now, you know, if you go into some groups they say, "You're bisexual, of course." You answer, "No, I'm not. I don't particularly like sucking cocks. I've nothing against it for those who like it but it's not my bag," and it's "Hummmph. Inferior type," right off the bat.

I've done just about everything, but I have to put a

slight disclaimer to that. It's like *Peer Gynt,* Ibsen's very
beautiful play, where Peer Gynt goes through life
devil-may-care. When he dies, he goes to hell and he
tells the Devil he'd like a nice little niche. But the
Devil says, "No. You weren't bad enough for hell and
you weren't good enough for heaven." Peer asks,
"What do you do?" "What they do with people like
you," the Devil answers, "is they take their souls and
they give them to the buttonmaker and he puts them
in a pot, melts them down, and makes new ones out of
them. This is for all the mediocre people."

So on one level I've done everything. I've gone
through Kraft-Ebbing and gone through Kinsey. I've
done it all at least once, with some notable exceptions.
I haven't killed anybody or been killed and there are
certain of the so-called perversions that I haven't
needed to do, but I've covered a broad spectrum. Yet
it's always been like a blushing virgin.

Right now I'm in a funny situation. My reputation
brings me to a point where people say, "An Erotic
Expert." But I've reached a stage in my life where
eroticism *per se* is no longer the blinding obsession
that it once was. There was a period of ten or fifteen
years where everything was incidental to fucking. You
exercised in order that your body would look good
and you could fuck better. You eat healthy foods so
that you can have more energy and fuck better. You
work in order to make money and decorate your pad
so you can lure people in to fuck better. It was all
centered on that. Being of a Neapolitan poetic nature,

I of course blew it up into an extraordinary personal opera: My Search For The Ultimate Orgastic Experience.

About a year ago, I said, "I really want to do the thing that's realest for me. I want to do the thing that will make me face me in my complete depth. I know I can dance around a lot, but can I really go deep?" So I decided to get married. That's been my Metasexual trip for the last year. I haven't had a Sexual trip in that we haven't been fucking to make a baby. But my Metasexual trip has been, by any standard, exemplary. It's been pristine. And the whole erotic experience is beginning to fall into place for me. I'm beginning to see it as, "Yes. It's definitely a very rich and good and beautiful part of life, but it's not going to save anybody."

Currently, I feel split. On the one hand I feel like I'm advertised in terms of Metasexuality yet I'm not dealing with that anymore in my personal life. So what I intend to do is talk about Metasexuality for a while and then make it open and personal and talk about life. Because when you get into life, you begin to understand where eroticism fits in the overall scheme of things.

2. CHILDHOOD AND ADOLESCENCE

MY MOTHER WILL KILL ME . . .

My first erotic experience occured when I was eight years old. The woman next door put her two-year-old daughter in our house and left for the store. My mother went shopping with her and left me alone with this girl. Now I'm thirty-seven, and I still wonder whether you should leave me alone in a room with a two-year-old girl.

I was building something with my erector kit, having good thoughts and being righteous, when I turned my head and there she was. A woman. Temptation.

She was lying there. You know how little babies are? They kick their legs and they thrash their arms and they stick their tongues out and they rub themselves. They're very, very erotic. She turned me on and I wanted to ball her. It's a very normal thing. As soon as I had that impulse—"Wouldn't it be good to go rub up against that little girl"—the first thought I had was, "If my mother catches me, she'll kill me." (I think, "Where does an eight-year-old kid learn that?" You don't have to learn wanting to rub up against a little girl. That's born in us. It's the right stuff, the natural stuff. That's God given. But the "My mother will kill me," that's what causes the neurosis and the armoring; all that stuff in the middle that we have to wade through in later life.)

So I thought, "The kid's two years old. She can't talk. So she won't be able to tell. By the time she grows up and is able to talk, she won't remember and by then it won't matter. And nobody else is in the house, so I can do it."

So what's dirty, man? There it was. The original dirty. Doing something that's forbidden; the apple that you're not supposed to eat. I went up to her and pulled down her diapers, fingers trembling, and really, really, really getting it on. And there it was. The cunt. Wow! A two-year-old kid.

I laid down next to her, positioned myself up

alongside her, and was rubbing against her and feeling good. I don't remember whether I had an erection or not, but it was just feeling nice. And she was cooing and gurgling and having a good time. We started to relax. Like you smoke a J, have a little wine and you get into it. When suddenly, Bam! The front door slams. My mother and the neighbor woman. Like the Gestapo. They're going to come in while we're doing this. So I get up, like, "Oh my God, it's my husband," pull up my pants and get the kid's diaper back on. They enter and the baby starts crying. I act very innocent, sitting there and playing once more with my erector kit. What am I supposed to know? I'm only eight years old. Isn't it amazing how smart you are at an early age? You've really got it all figured out by the time you're six or seven.

Later I thought, "That's the sort of thing that you think of as perverse." *Pedophilia,* they call it. That's dirty. You go to jail for it. You get twenty-five years. They lock you up and lay all kinds of shit on you and tell stories about you. About the Dirty Old Man. If you go to prison the other prisoners try to kill you because you're so low. Yet the kid didn't start crying until the mothers came in and laid a guilt trip on my psyche. Up until then it was fine. It was normal and natural and good.

Q: Maybe the baby started crying because you stopped.

M: I never considered it that way before.

DATING RITUALS . . .

Q: Do you believe in petting on the first date?

M: That was a very simple question when I was fifteen. Then it was all laid out quite clearly by a very
very strong cultural code. I grew up in a first- and
second-generation Italian neighborhood which is
very feudal and insular, where everybody knew
everybody else within a square mile. You couldn't do
anything in private. Maybe you could get off to the
cellar and jerk off, but you always had a suspicion that
somebody knew. Because at the very least, you had to
tell the priest.

If you went out on a date, the first one was in the
soda shop. Everyone hung about there and if you got
to like a particular girl you went up to her and asked,
"Would you like to go sit at a separate table with me?"
That was a very marked event. Everybody saw that. It
was noted.

Then you asked her to a movie to show your good
faith; that you were willing to spend money on her.
Afterwards you went for a hamburger and you took
her to her door. If you got a light peck-kiss on the lips
"good night," you were so far ahead of the game you
couldn't believe it. You were happy all week. Like,
"Wow! I'm moving forward at breakneck speed."

Next you would take her to a movie and you would
hold hands. You might put your arm around her and

you might get a vague brush of a breast through a taffeta blouse. By the fourth date you were ready to ask her to the Drive.

It was the East River Drive between 124th and 106th Streets. That was all East Harlem Italian turf. You could go anywhere in the neighborhood any hour of the day or night and be safe, because nobody was there but members of the Tribe, or the Nation. If you had a personal enemy, you had to watch out. If some specific individual had it in for you, you stayed away from dark places. Otherwise, if you had a poetic turn, as I did, you'd walk up and down the Drive pretending that you were there for the river or the moon.Then you'd sit down and put your arm around her. She would lean in a bit, you'd talk, and there'd be that electrifying moment when the whole Universe disappeared and you could kiss. It was legal and safe. There were people on other benches but you had paid your dues and followed the rules so you were allowed this and could enjoy it as much as you wanted.

You kept that up for three, four, five, or six weeks, depending on how it went. The big, big breakthrough was when she invited you to her house to baby-sit, for her parents were going to be out. Then you got to soul kiss and touch breasts and rub, hopefully, until you came. Because if you didn't come, she wasn't going to do anything. The longest this went on for me was about a year. Shortly after, I joined the air force.

The question now, should you pet on the first date? It's more like, should you fuck on the first date? That's the real question.

One of my fables in *The Erotic Comedies** asks the question, "Should you let someone shit in your mouth on the first date?" A little teen-aged girl asks her mother that question and her mother answers, "Well, you know in our day we'd wait until we were married. Not it's a more liberal age so you should at least wait until you're engaged." It's *reductio ad absurdum*. It brings out the ridiculous.

"To fuck or not to fuck" is a question that frequently arises. It happens a lot at the office where you meet somebody, look at each other, and like each other. Next thing you know you're conversing at the water cooler. Then you're having lunch together. Very rapidly, the issue arises. Nobody lays it on anybody, necessarily, but suddenly the possibility is there: Tarzan and Jane, and you've got to do something about it.

Whether or not it's on the first date, you take your pleasure and you take your chances. You can get in very very deeply with someone very quickly via the erotic chute and suddenly be in a place where you look around, wonder whether you want to be there, and it's too late. The bond's been made. Then there's no way out except by pain. I'm sure we've all experienced that, where it's no longer "do I want to get out

---

*The Erotic Comedies, by Marco Vassi, published by The Permanent Press, Sag Harbor, New York

or don't I?" but, "there are only two ways out: death
or divorce." One is fatal and the other painful.

There was a cartoon in *Playboy* depicting a church.
A wedding has just finished and the groom is there, in
a tuxedo, with his best friend standing next to him.
The groom says, "I don't know. I just wanted to get
laid and it got out of hand." So you've got to be
careful on the first date.

3. THE AIR FORCE AND COLLEGE

JAPAN . . .

I had joined the air force at nineteen, after leaving Iona College, and arrived in San Francisco a virgin. A cab driver turned me on to a whorehouse where I think, in my nervousness, I must have slipped my cock between a whore's thighs and come within thirteen seconds. I still don't know if I penetrated her, which left me wondering what it was all about, this fucking thing that I'd been looking forward to so much.

33

A week later I arrived in Japan, where prostitution was still legal. I get to the base, step out, and there are five hundred bars in a small area. Ten to fifty girls are in each one, ranging from the ugly to the ravishingly beautiful, all to be had for five to ten dollars. I fucked myself silly for the next two and a half years. That's all I did. I had a job translating Chinese language broadcasts, was writing letters home and had a full regular life. But the driving passion was fucking. That's all I thought about morning, noon, and night.

After two and a half years of this I was pretty tired and sick at heart, weary, homesick, drunk a lot, and wondering "What does it all mean? What am I doing?" when I went with a friend to the town of Fukuoka. He stopped to buy cigarettes. As this girl went to get his cigarettes he took off his sun glasses, looked into them and realized his image was upside down. She saw him seeing that, giggled, I said something to her in Japanese and we began to talk in broken English and broken Japanese. We liked each other and I asked her to have dinner.

This was very rare, for a nice Japanese girl to go out with an American serviceman. It was frowned upon, but you could do it if you showed you weren't a barbarian who wanted nothing but to drink, fuck, and ravish the country. So all through dinner I'm the nice guy; the young, Italian, Catholic boy. I'm polite and I'm speaking about culture and my interest in Buddhism, all the while thinking, "Oh, boy. I'm going to fuck her. And she's not a whore. She's probably a virgin." I'm really digging that, because I've never fucked a woman simply because she liked me. Some of the whores I went to bed with got to like me and vice versa, but this was the real thing. Whoring is sinful and not real but this is the way I was told, as a kid, it's supposed to be.

By the end of dinner I'm coming on, making eyes, and she gets a little nervous. I take her to a movie and I try to hold her hand. At the end of the date she tells me, "Look. I like you a lot but you make me very nervous. Let me introduce you to Yoshie."

Yoshie is a good looking, very hip gal, totally Japanese, but she would have loved to come to America, smoke grass, get drunk, ball an American, and taste strange things in life. Yet she was very timid. We'd get into very heavy necking, but she wouldn't let me even touch her under her brassiere. We struggled for about two months. It was East Harlem all over again. Then she said, "I'll introduce you to my oldest sister." The chain, right? And she introduces me to Hatsue.

Hatsue is three years older than I am and teaches kindergarten. She's a Methodist and was taught English by missionaries. She's taller than most Japanese with a broad face, having some Russian blood in her. And she's a virgin. We started dating and I get involved. All of the remorse, loneliness, fears and homesickness comes to the surface, because she's really taking care of me, wanting to see that I eat well, and such. But it was very non-erotic. I never had a hard-on for her. I never looked at her with an "Oh, boy. I really want to fuck her." Not that she wasn't an attractive woman. She was, but I had no lust for her. She was a "nice girl."

We finally decide to go to bed. I'm feeling that I don't know what I'm getting into, but I'm still going to the whorehouses, beginning to feel bad about it, and thinking I should straighten up and get serious with Hatsue. So it's time to ball.

The first time we try it it's in a friend's rented house in the village nearby; whores all around and kids screaming. It was a very raucous scene and I'm totally impotent. Which is to be expected. How am I going to fuck this nice girl in the middle of the degeneracy of my life? I'm depressed for a week because I couldn't get it up and talk to a good friend about it. He was an older man and pooh-poohed it. "Of course. What did you expect? Next time do it right. Spend the night."

So we went to this beautiful Japanese inn that came out of a Kurosawa movie. Sliding doors. Tatamis. We enter our room. The maid comes in walking on her knees—really traditional, because she doesn't want to be equal to the guests. There's a perfect rock garden outside. We're told that our bath is ready. We come out of the bath, everything is put away, and there are two mats on the floor six inches apart. "Why are they pushed apart?" I ask. "Why are they not together?" "The management does not wish to suggest that anything improper will take place here tonight," she answers.

The place was called *Mimatsue*—whispering pines— and at one point I wrote a haiku, in Japanese. In my excitement I rushed up to Hatsue and said, "Look! I wrote a haiku, one of the most difficult art forms to master. I wrote it in Japanese and it contains a play on words!" And she said, "It's not right. You can't do it that way." I wondered, "How did I ever feel anything for this woman?" She was faultless in her demeanor and behavior and totally without passion.

Anyway, we go to bed, I think I had an erection, and I think there was penetration, although I don't actually remember it. It was all so under the sheets and nobody wanted to look. It was weird. The most obscure fuck I had ever had. In the morning there was blood on the sheets. I was convinced she put chicken blood on the sheet in order to make me feel that I had broken her maidenhood the night before. I'll never know, of course. Then, naturally, I had to marry the girl. I'd taken her virginity. I was, realize, twenty-two years old. I'd gone from East Harlem to Japan, spent two years the whorehouses, but had never been intimate in the "real" way.

I announced my intentions and asked if she wanted to marry me. She said, "I have to think about it. It sounds absolutely insane." But finally she accepted.

I fought the air force for three months. I fought the embassy. I fought everybody. They threw me out of the security service. My best friends, the chaplain, the major, my parents (I had written them), people on the street, her friends, my friends, they all said, "Don't do this. It's a mistake. It's obvious to the entire race that what you two people are intending to do is ill advised. No matter what you two think about it, please take the advice of the collective species, which says, unanimously and in a loud voice, 'It's a mistake.'" No! I pull my samurai sword and charge ahead. We get married.

First we get married at the embassy, for I'm an American citizen. By this time I'm working in the laundry room, because they took away my security clearance. I had gone from top-secret translator of Chinese—an electronic spy—to folding sheets and dirty laundry, because of my supposed love for this woman. But we do it. We're in the embassy, sign the papers, walk out, and it's a beautiful day. There's a lake and there are people and there are trees. I'm walking one or two steps behind her. I pause, midstep, my heart literally sinks into my stomach, and I realize, "I didn't want to do that. I don't want to undertake the pledge." Of course, the next thing I did was to go ahead with the religious ceremony, at a church, where I dressed as a samurai warrior. That finished, I thought, "This is getting sillier and sillier. I just don't want to be doing this thing."

It comes time to be leaving for America and she can't come with me. She comes to Tokyo with me where we had a great sobbing, because of the heartbreak of "*Sayonara,* the Japanese Goodbye." We're at the airport, I'm in the men's room, and her brother comes in. I'm sitting there and he says, "You know, she's crying."

"Well," I answered, "that's the way with women."

He looks down at me and says, "Is not the heart of Vassisan touched also?"

The dialogue was out of a movie. "Do you not feel the pang of sorrow and separation?" And the tears just welled out. I'm sitting in the bathroom sobbing disconsolately. I finish crying, come out, and it's "Goodbye . . . goodbye." I get on the plane and heave a sigh of relief.

Two and a half years in the Orient and now I'm going home. But I don't know where home is. Kennedy had been elected president. Who knew who Kennedy was? I read Jack Kerouac when I left to go to Korea, years earlier, *On The Road*. I didn't know what I was coming back to. I return to New York, see people, my parents are living in a new place, I'm going to start Brooklyn College in a month, I look up an old girlfriend and cha-cha-cha. I've really got it together, because I'm going to go to the campus with all these eighteen-year-olds and I'm twenty-three. Then my mother taps me on the shoulder and says, "Oh, by the way, didn't you get married?"

"Oh, right. I got married."

"Well you've got to bring her over here, don't you?"

"Huh?" I didn't really want to bring her over. But the voice of tradition and responsibility called; being true to your promise and your word. So the next act began.

My parents loaned me money, I mail the money to Hatsue, and the minute she steps off the plane I again feel, "God. I don't know what I'm going to do with her. I don't want her to be here." My parents set up a reception. Friends come and the best man and the family and the tuxedos. People brought presents,

everyone goes home, and now I'm living in this pad
on Ninetieth Street with her. I'm going to Brooklyn
College in the day, at night I'm working as a file clerk
at ASCAP, and I'm living with this Japanese woman.
And I'm not hip enough to have the terminology for
it.

I can't say to myself, "It's absurd. It's absurdist life
drama." Or, "This is Metatheater." Nor can I get any
kind of a fix on it which will make me comfortable;
make me laugh or happy with it. Instead, it gets
weirder and weirder. I get sick, collapse at ASCAP,
and a friend brings me home. I vomit bile for twenty-
four hours. I've got to go to my parents' house. I'm
afraid I'm going to die. I've been at school for eight
hours and at work for six hours, I'm vomiting green
shit, worrying, trying to get a marriage together and I
can't do it. In fact, I'm dying from the attempt. Just
then, Hatsue comes in and gives me head. It's the last
thing I wanted. I wanted to recuperate. But she had
never done that before and this is a really precious
gift she wanted to give me because I'm sick. So I
accepted it and I started to get better. She gave me the
gift of head and it cured me.

I recover and we're going to move to Queens and
get a new start. My uncle and aunt own a building and
give us the bottom flat. My father comes, rips it apart
and puts it back together again. The kitchen is
painted with gold leaf around the moldings. He's
created the painter's masterpiece for his son, when
again, everyone goes home.

By then, I'm hanging out with a bunch of commu-

nists—George and Julie and Ray. They're living on
Atlantic Avenue and are really hip. It's revolution,
man, and they've got a commune. They call it The
First Williamsburgh Soviet. There are secret and forbidden books; Marx and Engels and Trotsky. There's
talk of blowing up the banks and Pete Seeger records;
songs of the Spanish Fifth Brigade and all the rest.
And at Brooklyn College, I'm failing at one course
and another course.

The most brilliant psychology professor comes up
to me the first day of courses, takes me aside, and
says, "You obviously know much more than anything
we can teach you through this course. So don't worry
about anything for the rest of the year. You have an
A." This was after talking to me for five minutes.
Meanwhile, I soon start to fail everything else. The
woman who was to become my first therapist—who
also taught a psychology course—is seducing me, telling me I'm falling apart; that I'm held together with
spit and why don't I fuck my mother like I was supposed to when I was a kid. This chaos and excitement
again brought me to, "I don't want to be living in
Queens, married to this Japanese Methodist. I'm a
kid. I'm young. I want to revolutionize the world and
turn it upside down. And I had met the Marilyn
Monroe of Brooklyn College and was after her. So I
had to get rid of my wife.

I was sorry. I liked her a lot. It was comfortable and
I could see how it was really good, but I'm being
pulled by something—by passion. So there are
months of fights; that phase of it where she literally

could not say to me "Pass the salt," without it being a pretext for some kind of warfare. Finally, I decided I had to take it on myself and that if I wanted out, I had to do it myself. I couldn't bank on her to do it for me.

She went out one day. I calmly packed the few clothes I felt I owned and a book or two in a case. I felt hungry, looked around, fried two frankfurters in butter, washed the pan, hung it up, felt almost smug about how little I was feeling—I was so dispassion-ate—and moved into the communist commune.

There were a series of afterwaves; of aftershocks. The decision was done but there was profound guilt for having brought her from Japan and what would she do now? Months of incoherent feelings. We saw each other progressively less. After two years I would call her every three months to see how she was, and then she left for Japan.

Later, my mother got a note that she had married, and the guilt lifted. I felt that whatever loop I put her on, she was back on some sort of track. A year and and half later my mother received another card say-ing that Hatsue had given birth to a son. Then it was totally over. She was back.

But I had done penance for many years up to that point. I didn't beat my breast or put ashes in my hair, or tell anyone how I was suffering because I felt I had mistreated my wife. But I felt that I had committed a sin.

ASS-MAN . . .

What's the old category? Ass-men, tit-men, leg-men? When you throw out the cliche, sometimes you throw out the wisdom of the cliche. Certain cliches have a great truth in them. People really do respond to each other on the basis of the most obscure thing. At school I knew a Platonic scholar who actually received his Ph.D. in Plato. He was a truly brilliant man and one of the few people I knew who spoke in complete paragraphs with footnotes. If you wanted to talk with Steve, you had to really pay attention, because you had to follow every sentence in the paragraph. If you didn't get the whole paragraph, you didn't get the thought. And if you missed the footnotes, you missed the richness and the humor. You know how scholars are. They make these very dry, obscure jokes in the footnotes. Steve was the most ethereal, fantastic person; really big-domed, with a Webster type forehead and all. And he fell for Jackie.

Jackie was French, and a most tight chick. That's not a pejorative term, merely descriptive. There are women and there are ladies and females and those of the cunty gender who can be all of these roles at different times. But this one was a "chick." That was her role. The way she walked and the tight skirts and the tension in the lips and the razor eyes and all the rest of it. It was fearsome. Like spokes on the old Roman chariot. You didn't want to go too close to her because she'd chop you up. Of all the people in the world for poor, innocent, Platonic Steve to fall for, it was Jackie. She was working in the office he worked in and I was Steve's rommate at the time.

We used to spend our evenings talking about Greek philosophers and eating TV dinners. It was a nice time and I look back upon it fondly. One night he came home and he said, "I'm in love with this girl."

"Oh. Far out," I said.

He paused and answered, "To be precise, I'm in love with this girl's ass."

"That's kind of cool. That happens to all of us."

And he said, "More than anything in the world, I want to fuck her in the ass."

"What's so strange?" I asked, and then I realized he was making one of the Platonic Absolutes out of her ass. There it was. The Good. The True. The All-in-One ass. But he didn't know how to get past the spokes and the razor blades, so he courted her for six months.

It was true courtship, He gave her flowers and he sent her poems and he took her out for dinners and movies and plays and opened to her the entire world of scholarship and intellectual cerebration. She was quite taken by this. It really touched her and she was warmed and said, "Gee. You've opened a whole world for me." It was a classic love story and resulted in marriage.

They fucked before they got married. It got to the point where they did go to bed, but he couldn't bring himself to say to her, "Hey. I'd like to fuck you in the ass." They were married for about a year. They balled and had fights and did all the things that married couples do with this great unspoken thing between the two of them. Finally, at the end of the year, he said to her, "I'd like to fuck you in the ass." She answered, matter-of-factly, "Okay," as women at times are wont to respond. "We'll give it a try."

He fucked her in the ass, came, and said that immediately after the orgasm, she disappeared. Because she, as she was, never really existed. The only thing that existed was the vision that he was following, which was embodied by his desire to do that act. The minute the act was completed, the vision disappeared and suddenly he was with this strange female creature in his bed who was married to him.

Again, you've got to be careful.

ASS-WOMAN . . .

There was a girl who had the biggest ass at Brooklyn College. Brooklyn College had about twenty-thousand people in attendance when I was there and to be known as the girl with the biggest ass among twenty-thousand was a distinction of no small magnitude. She was heavier than the Dean. The Dean was the Dean, but she was the star of the campus. It was just one of those extraordinary anatomical whimsies that nature throws in every now and then.

She was a medium sized girl, about five foot five, with a normal size torso and breasts. Emerging from this body was this incredible monument. If it had been a little off here or there you would have said, "Gee. The poor thing. She's got a hump, or something"—the way you'd talk about a hunchback. But it was so perfect that as she'd walk by there'd be an audible "Ah!" You'd be in the cafeteria and there'd be five hundred to one thousand people drinking coffee and talking about Kant. She'd walk through and Kant went out the window because something much more profound was coming by.

I had a unique status at Brooklyn College. I had joined the air force, was twenty-three, and was "old" and experienced. I had done all these things and had a definite edge on all the eighteen- and nineteen-year-olds. Most of them hadn't been laid yet and they were still trying to grope around. And here I was with Japan and Korea under my belt.

So she became my target. I had to have the girl with the biggest ass in Brooklyn College.

I played it very, very, very suave. I pointedly pretended not to notice her. It took her about three months to notice that I was not noticing her. Because it was a big campus. But finally she realized that this older man, who was rumored to have learned all kinds of erotic techniques in the Far East, wasn't noticing her. I became, of course, irresistible.

We went out a couple of times and we necked and what have you. I was still very shy and awkward. For all my experience of walking into a whorehouse and saying, "Here's the money, you give me the girl," and you walk into a room and do it, I didn't know how to negotiate the human aspect of the thing. It was "There's that ass and here's this cock, but how do I obtain that specific goal?"

So we would talk and go out and kiss and neck a bit; the things we used to do in college. And one night I finally arranged to get her to my apartment. That was another thing. Most of the other guys were living at home, with their parents. But I had a job and money saved up so I had my own place.

The two of us are finally alone, I close the door, and I think, "Gee. I've got to neck with her and then I've got to fuck her and then I've got to get to know her for awhile and I've got to go through all these things before I can get what I want, which is to fuck her in the ass. How am I ever going to negotiate that?" I had never done that before in my life. They are very prim in Japan. Yet I had to get to this rank perversion, though I didn't know how.

We're sitting around and we're talking and she looks a little nervous. We talk a bit more when she clears her throat and says, "I hope you don't mind what I'm about to say."

"I can't imagine what it's going to be. Go ahead and say it."

"Do you mind? I only like to be fucked in the ass."

I thought, "It can't be true. There's got to be a catch somewhere. God's playing a joke. It's some sort of little karmic trick. It can't possibly be." So I hemmed and hawed about it, for when something's so good,

you really want to examine it before you take a bite
out of it. But she averred how that indeed was the
case; that this was precisely what she wanted and
nothing else. So I said, "The pleasure's mine, my
dear." I went ahead and did this deed and it was
really nice. Fucking is always nice and ass fucking has
its own particular kind of pleasure. And this was like
fucking a myth—not just an ass—it was a great mythic
structure and it was really good.

We got it on for awhile. After the fifth or sixth time,
one begins to get bored, to say, "That's very nice, but
isn't there more to this relationship?" Because we'd go
back to my apartment, she'd get undressed, I'd get
undressed, she'd lie down, I'd fuck her in the ass,
she'd get dressed, I'd get dressed, and she'd go home.
It got to where there wasn't enough sustaining the
central act for the central act to have any meaning. So
eventually I asked, "Why don't we try something
else?"

"Horrors," she said, lifting up her Victorian skirt.
She was shocked. I wanted to fuck her where it's
traditionally done and she was acting like I was some
kind of pervert.

So we hassled and hassled and hassled. Finally I got
the story out of her, which was one of those horror
stories. She was Jewish, brought up in Germany, and
her uncle was in the S.S.—one of those double in-
former type things. Anyway, he was a baddie who had
all sorts of dealings with the Germans. He was turning people in and all kinds of crap. The benefit of this
was that ultimately she got out of Germany and didn't

wind up dead. But because the uncle kept the family alive, her mother and father looked sidewise while the uncle was taking this little girl, who was her, and doing all kinds of nasty things to her in the cellar with the German equivalent of Coke bottles. One of the things he used to do was to whip her with his shirt, which must have been an army shirt because it had metal buttons on it. He would whip her with this shirt and then stick things in her ass, whereby the fetish. So she grew up with this. The ambivalence was that getting whipped with the metal buttoned shirt and having things shoved up her ass saved her life. It was a very heavy tale and I didn't know how to handle it. It was a little too much for a twenty-three-year-old psych major. All I wanted to do was get laid. I wasn't up for this historical drama.

One day, when she suggested that if I really cared for her I would go find a shirt with metal buttons on it, I freaked and split and didn't really see her any-more. I'd see her on campus but our relationship was over.

CRAZY GIRL . . .

The amusing thing in all this was that I was seeing another girl at the same time who was crazy. The kind of crazy she was, you'd go to bed and you'd be has-

sling, having some kind of fight, and she'd start getting weird. Her eyes would go funny and she'd stare
off into space and she'd get this strange smile on her
face. She'd pick up a butcher knife and start sharpen-
ing it. Going crazy like someone out of *Snakepit;* like
an imitation of someone going crazy. You knew that a
large part of it was a drama that she was mounting,
but she had a knife in her hands and you didn't know
how far she was going to carry her particular vision of
the universe in relation to somebody else's life.

I'd think, "Okay. I'm tired. I'm going to bed." Then
she'd come to bed, she has the knife with her, and
she'd be mumbling to herself. Mumble, mumble,
mumble. I'd wonder, "What are the chances, during
the night, that she's going to stick that thing in me?
Maybe ten percent? But that's pretty high." So I had
difficulties with her.

As fate would have it, the two of them met one
night. I was with the girl with the ass, having run away
from Barbara, the Crazy. I had been living with a
bunch of Marxists on Atlantic Avenue in Brooklyn
Heights. We were reading Marx and Lenin and preparing to enlighten the masses and all. But I ran away
from there, stayed with a friend for awhile, and took
the girl with the ass there one night. We're getting it
on when Barbara calls. She says to me, "I know where
you are and I'm coming to get you." I turned to this
other lady and I said, "Look. Somebody's coming over
soon and it can be a very very bad scene. We've got to
leave."

But by this time she's undressed and she's lying on

the couch like something out of Goya and flaunting her charms. I'm thinking, "I want to have both. I want to do the thing and I want to have safety, too." Lust and compassion running neck and neck. I thought, "Brooklyn Heights. It takes her five minutes to walk to the subway, an eight-minute subway ride, and an eight-minute walk by the time she gets here, into the building and into the elevator. I've got twenty-one minutes." I shave two minutes off because I don't want to meet her in the lobby. A nineteen-minute talk, preparation, stroke, foreplay, ass-fuck, get the clothes on, "Can't explain now but we've got to get out . . . Yes, yes, I know. I'm being very very quick and rushing the entire thing but we've got to get out," into the elevator, down the elevator, out into the lobby, we step into the lobby and she's there. She's standing there and her arms, up to the elbows, are cut. She's dripping blood, her hair is all frizzled, she's got the look in her eye, and she's carrying the knife—one of those big eighteen-inch butcher knives.

She looks up and says, "The first thing I'm going to do is kill the bitch." Poor girl. She got out of Nazi Germany by having things shoved up her ass, she doesn't need this. Here's this madwoman coming at her with an eighteen-inch butcher knife for no reason she can fathom. She came up to get laid, she's on her way home, she's being rushed, and suddenly this maniac is threatening her life. So I jump on the maniac.

We're wrestling with the knife and I've got her hand and we dance out into the street. I think it was Eighty-fifth Street. We're in the middle of a street where everybody is walking their poodles and doing their Upper East Side Eighty-fifth Street number— me and this girl in the middle of the road—with the knife up in the air and the blood, and this girl with the big ass standing on the stoop. Finally, in one of those blessed moments of quick thinking, I said to Barbara, "Look. If the cops come, we'll both be in trouble."

"Cops?" she asked.

"Right. Cops. We're dancing around in the middle of Eighty-fifth Street, you're bleeding, we've got a knife and they'll think I'm trying to kill you. They'll shoot me and the bullets will fly and you may get shot, too."

And suddenly it all drops. She kind of collapses, the knife falls to the ground, I pick up the knife, throw it off to the side, and now I've got these two women on my hands. Somehow I've got to do something with the two of them that makes it all turn out all right for everybody. But it's so split—it's all going in such opposite directions so rapidly and so massively—that I don't know how.

I hailed a cab, figuring that I'd just take everyone home. In those days that was the solution to everything. You took them home and what happened to them then was their problem. When we get in the cab, Barbara starts mumbling to herself and the other girl's getting hysterical. The cab driver is this guy of about seventy; a sweet old man, driving a cab, just trying to make a living. He looks in the back seat and what he sees there is sheer, raving madness. He doesn't know what it is, it's so crazy. Blood, people talking and screaming, and lust and fear. I'm saying, "Brooklyn Heights," for I'm going to drop Barbara off first.

He's driving and getting very nervous. The other girl's saying, "Take us to the hospital. Take us to the hospital. She's bleeding to death. Take her to the hospital" I'm saying, "It's okay. It's just a superficial wound. It's okay. It's just a superficial wound." We're going down the East Side Highway and after about five minutes the guy looked over his shoulder, very timidly, and asks, "What happened?"

I really don't know how to explain it to him and the other girl is in no mood to talk. Barbara suddenly sits up straight, this gleam of rational lucidity comes into her eyes, she leans over, smiles very sweetly, and says, "It's my birthday. We were having a party. I went to cut the cake and the knife slipped. That's what happened." And we rode all the way to Atlantic Avenue in this incredible stunned silence. Nobody wanted to say another word. The thought was, "Let's just get through it." I got both of them home and it all turned out more or less all right.

I don't know what happened to the other girl, but I ran into Barbara a year or two ago. I'm walking down Sixth Avenue, as is my wont, trying to figure it out and figure it out and think my way through and I hear someone say, "Hello Fred"—which used to be my name. I turned around and I'm confronted with this black woman who looks like Aunt Jemima. It's Barbara. She's just gotten moon-faced, very big and very jolly. It was "Ho ho ho ho! Ho ho ho ho!" from this big, fat, jolly woman.

The entire past leaped into my mind. She comes up, kisses me on the cheek, embraces me and says, quite boisterously, "How are you?" Like somebody who finds Jesus, she had undergone that total transformation of personality. The insanity, neurosis, all of it gone. We talked a bit about the old days. She's living in Rhode Island and tells me to "drop me a line sometime." "You're on," I answered, and later I sent her a copy of *The Saline Solution*.

There is a chapter in that book which describes the story I just told. As has happened many times in my life, she wrote back a note saying, "I was very amused by it, but nothing at all like that happened." It wasn't, "It was a little bit exaggerated," but "Nothing like that happened." So it all sails off into the void.

PSYCHOTHERAPY . . .

One of my great therapeutic insights happened when I was twenty-four—after the air force and the girl with the ass. I was extremely intelligent and sophisticated, except that I fell apart. So I went into therapy with "S". I won't say the name because she's still doing therapy. S was a nice lady, about forty-five, plump and pleasant and hip and all the rest, who developed a lech for me because I was in her psychology class. One day, after class, she called me aside and said, "Come with me. We'll do therapy." "Okay. Because I'm falling apart anyway."

We start doing breathing and relaxation therapy. One thing leads to another, and the next thing you know I'm balling my therapist. We're sitting and talking one day and she asked, "Did you ever catch or hear your parents fuck?" I thought about it for a moment and said, "No. I never did."

"Where was your bedroom?"

"Next to theirs. We lived in a four room flat. Their bedroom, mine, and a living room and a kitchen."

"Was there a door?" she asked.

"There was a doorway but no door."

"You mean," she continued, "that you slept in the next room for nineteen years and you never heard them fuck?"

"No. I never did."

"Well, did you hear anything?"

"Yeah," I answered. "I remember one night when I woke up because I heard something."

"What did you hear?"

"I heard my mother going "OOOHHH! OOOOHHHH! OOOOHHHH! OOOOHHHH! OOOOOOHHHHHH! OOOHHH!" Then my father said, "JEAN! JEAN! JEAN!." I got very frightened and I sat up in bed and said, "MA! MA! WHAT's WRONG?" And my father said, "Go back to sleep. Your mother's having a nightmare."

My dear therapist looked back at me in loving

disbelief for a full sixty seconds—I guess that's why she fell in love with me because I was the most naive person she had ever seen—and she said, "You believed him?"

"Yeah. Of course." And then a slow realization came over me and I said, "You don't mean that they were FUCKING, do you?" And that's what you go to therapy for; to realize that you're twenty-four years old and you've never emotionally admitted to yourself that your mother was there with her legs in the air and fighting and screeching and yelling and calling out just like any other woman does. And your father was getting it on, not only like any other man does it, but probably an awful lot like you do it.

That's happened to me a number of times. We turn into our parents a lot. We're sitting there and we say, "Wow! This is the way my father used to sit." A number of times, while fucking, I'd think, "This is probably just the way he used to do it."

Q: Do you think it would be harmful if your child saw you fuck?

M: The thing with kids and fucking is, "No. It's not a nightmare and it's not shameful and it's not where you should make a program out of it where you tie your kid to a chair and make him watch you fuck because he should know that." But you let your kid know. He'll find out.

My parents used to call me *brugia fiero,* which means "iron burner," because I was so mischievous I'd

burn iron. The other name they had for me was
petrozina, which means "parsley." It came from the
phrase *petrozina mizza la minestra*. Which means "parsley inside the spinach." There was an Italian way of
cooking spinach in which you'd put the parsley inside.
I'm told—I don't remember this—that came about
because up until the age of six or seven, when I'd
wake up in the morning, I'd crawl into their bed and
sleep between the two of them. What a fantastically
beautiful thing that must have been to have people
that you love and you wake up and get into bed with
them. To think of what we've made BED in our time.
Then you get into culture comparisons—like the Chinese, where they all sleep on the hearth.

Sometimes I think, "What do I have against marriage?" I'm married, but there are things about it that
I don't like. And one objection I have to it as a form is
that there tends to be that lack of people just being
able to lie together. Because the family's too small. It's
become two. You leave home, find a woman or a man,
and you duplicate the nuclear arrangement that you
came from. You become your parents. If you just
have people you can sleep with and lie down with,
they're your family, because you love them and you're
warm and all the rest. You can't get into bed with
anyone anymore unless you're going to be fucking.
And that's a real shame.

4. A YOUNG MAN'S EXPLORATIONS

THE BATHS . . .

Q. What have the baths meant to you?

M: There are a number of bath houses in town. In fact, the great majority of them are essentially gay houses, in which men go to meet other men for erotic reasons. They range from the Felliniesque—like the St. Mark's Baths, which are grungy and dirty and perverse and have all kinds of strange types hanging

out there—to the Continental, which has rock con-
certs and Bette Midler and pretty boys and everybody's dancing and everyone's happy happy happy all
the time.

At the St. Mark's nobody's ever happy. You go there
and it's very grim. You do your best but nobody has
too good a time about it. Serious fags only; no fucking
around. It's not for kids. They go to the Club Baths,
which caters to a young and college crowd. There it's
"Tennis anyone?" All these twenty-two-year-old butch
types walking down the hallway looking like they want
to play football. Then there's the Eberhard, which has
a reputation for being an S&M (sado-masochism)
B&D (bondage and discipline) place. You go there
and look into a room and there's a guy lying handcuffed. You ask yourself, "What does this guy want?
Why is this man lying there naked and handcuffed?
He obviously wants something. His door is opened.
What can I give him?" And you think. "Does he want
me to kick him in the head? Does he want me to suck
his cock? Does he want me to shove my fist up his
ass?" It's a funny thing in our day of great liberation
that most of the time you don't feel you can ask—that
you have to figure it out somehow instead of going in
and saying, "Hey. What do you want?"

There are the Mt. Morris baths up at 125th Street
in Harlem, which I've been told is a ninety-five percent black bath. And whatever it is that that particular
subcultural twist gives it, goes on up there. So these
are the baths. Finally, there is one Russian Bath on the
Lower East Side which consists mostly of men sitting

about talking of how they're going to lose their pot bellies and about the queers who go to the St. Mark's Baths. These guys eat food and do a very heavy male number. They sweat a lot and say things like "I took steam five times today."

In terms of interest, I'd rank the baths on a level with the Grand Canyon. Both are total phenomena that could hold your attention for a long time. I could probably sit and look at the Grand Canyon for ten years without any trouble. And the baths have been like that.

I don't think there's a similar thing for women that's quite like that, where you can just go and put on a towel and cruise for some kind of fucking or sucking or whatever you want to do. If I'm mistaken, somebody tell me, because it's the best kept secret in town.

If we lived in a healthier society we'd be out in the fields cutting corn and singing like the Russian Chorus. But we don't have those kinds of outlets. We go to the office and shuffle papers and so we get into our manhood marches erotically.

The baths, for those of you who haven't been there, are our equivalent of the grain-field. You go in, strip down, put on the towel, and you're ready to do battle. I'd go to these places stoned—do some grass, or maybe a little mescaline, or sniffing poppers, and "going out there and going out there and going out there." There'd be incredible thoughts where the mind begins to gallop and you begin to subsume larger and larger universes. I'm sure that many of you have had these moments of, "Wow! It suddenly opens up." Your mind expands and it finally takes the entire universe in. There it was before my eyes. The Ultimate. The erotic and mental spheres coming together. Then "Pop!" It just disappeared like a bubble, and I would be back in this actual reality.

So from where I can see, you're not going to get any kind of metaphysical, spiritual or other kind of insight through that particular Metasexual trip which is going to be of any but peripheral value.

EVERYBODY'S GOT A STORY . . .

One night in the baths I walked past a room and there were three men inside. One guy was lying on the bed giving head to the guy who was standing up next to him while the guy behind him was fist-fucking him. It was absolutely incredible. I glanced in and there was this super-Felliniesque tableau going on. The energy was just electric. It was curling the paint off the walls. Because there was this incredible force of putting a fist in somebody's asshole and all the energy that was going in that end was coming out the other end to the head that he was giving to the guy who was standing up. I looked at that and thought, "I've never done anything like that. I've never been fist fucked or had that kind of incredible thing happening. Who is this guy lying on the bed? Tomorrow does he go into an office or to the school or wherever he works wearing a suit? And talks, like all the rest? When the night before this extraordinary event was occuring?"

A few nights ago I was visiting a friend. A guy from her office had driven her home. He's fifty-five years old, balding, very meek, and looks like he's never done anything more exciting than crossing against the light. We started talking when he took out some photographs of himself. He used to be one of the prime skaters with Sonja Henne and the old *Ice Capades*. There are pictures of him in skin-tights, whirling and flashing about on the ice. And I thought, "Jesus. Everyone's got a story."

FILTH AND DEGRADATION . . .

Q: Some of the events you describe sound quite filthy. You're not suggesting that a fist in the ass is the thing to do, are you?

M: I began writing as a pornographer five years ago, and I still think in terms that many would consider obscene. I like filth.

Q: What does filth mean to you?

M: Filth has to do with a mood, a feeling, an internal
sense. It doesn't necessarily have to do with behavior.
You can pee in somebody's mouth and it doesn't have
to be filthy. It can be a loving thing. On the other
hand, you can be in the most chaste, connubial em-
brace, and it can be really dirty.

I had an affair with a man, a dirty old man of about
sixty-five, who was really lascivious and lecherous and
ugly and filthy. You look at him and you say, "Oh,
God. It's a dirty old man." If you walked down the
street, he would appear like someone in a L'il Abner
cartoon, with "Dirty Old Man" written over his head.

I met him at the St. Mark's Baths. He was a ticket
taker. He took your money and gave you a room
number. I was into a period where I wanted to explore debasement and degradation. I wanted to find
out what that was all about. Everybody, I think, has a
certain feeling of, "If I could only meet someone who
would make me crawl."

Bill was old. He had lost his sexual enthusiasm. He
just had a taste. But I was young, very energetic, and
talented.

I used to go to his place, a furnished room on East
Sixth Street. The superintendent was deaf, so you
had to pound on the door and ring the bell. And the
superintendent knew what you were there for. You
were going up to see the dirty old man and he knew
all the things you were going to be doing up there. So
the minute you walked into the place you began to
feel it. You began to feel that deep, dirty thrill that just

goes right down to your asshole, of "Oh, God. It's going to be good."

I'd go up there and he'd open the door. He'd be dressed in a bathrobe. It was a musty, furnished room. You couldn't make any noise, because the walls were very thin. And we did strange things.

He'd hit me with a belt. Or drop burning wax on my nipples, which was very interesting. It's a level of pain where you think, "Oh, Jesus! I won't be able to take this." But the wax cools immediately, and it doesn't damage you. So anybody who's into S&M and recognizes the difference between pain and damage (pain, you know, never hurt anybody; it's the damage that does the damage, as it were) can appreciate it. I met one guy who wanted to put metal clips on my nipples and send a 220 volt charge through. And I thought, "I don't think so."

Bill was into cutting me with knives and that sort of thing, which was the furthest end of the spectrum that I wished to explore. He constantly asked me, "When are you really going to do it? When are you going to stop playing around?" Because we'd get into a little whipping, and I'd pull back with a posed "Ooooohh!" And he'd say, "When are you really going to feel the pain of the thing?" I'd squirm and be girlish and he'd ask, "That's all very cute, but when are you going to be the thing you want to be?"

Or we'd get into urinary games. I'd be there in the shower and he'd be ready for it all and I'd protest, "Oh! Don't pee on me/Yes, do/Don't pee on me/Yes,

do." That kind of thing. He kept saying, "Look. Do
you want to drink piss or don't you? What are you
doing here? If you're a piss drinker, we'll get on with
it. And if you're not, why are you doing this thing?"
I'd answer, "I'm only here for the experience."

The thing with Bill, though, was that after a while
we began to have a really loving relationship. At the
beginning, when I went up there, neither one of us
would talk or look at each other because it would be a
dirty thing. But after a while, when you have Metasex
with somebody, you get to know them. He told me
about his life and I told him about mine. We got to
lending each other money. And then he began to get
into his loneliness. That was very moving. We'd sit
and talk. I'd cry and he'd cry. He'd say, "You know,
I've got nobody to talk to, nobody to really tell about
myself." So we'd have these really beautiful moments.

Interestingly, my father's name is Bill. We'd do a lot
of the scenarios: Master/slave and dog/owner (where
he'd put the dog collar on me). One night he said, "Do
you want to do father/son?" Everybody's got a thing
with their parents, of course, so we got into this
number. I was giving him head and he said, "That's it,
son. Suck your father's cock." What with his name, the
entire event came together. I thought, "Talk about
Freudianism. If I were to share this with a group of
psychoanalysts, they'd say it was sick." Yet it's the
essence of what analysis is about. People go to analysts
and never get that type of therapeutic catharsis.

The story has a sad ending. I lost touch with Bill
and then called him one day. The people where he

worked said he was sick and he'd been put in Bellevue. He was catatonic and then he was paranoid.
Simply put, he was just falling apart. When I called
Bellevue to find out how he was, they said that he had
died. They asked me if I knew any relatives, because
they were holding the body for burial. I wanted to say,
"Me. I'm his son," but you can't make that kind of a
jump.

Wilhelm Reich talked about how, "underneath
every bit of distorted, grotesque behavior, I always
found a little bit of human simplicity." And it's true.
When you go into the heart of that which seems most
repugnant to you, if you come out the other side
you'll always find goodness. You always find something beautiful. If you get through. Sometimes it kills
you, trying to get through.

SIMULTANEOUS AFFAIRS . . .

*Q: I need a comfortable new sex partner that I can return to
by choice, rather than commitment. I need to have multiple,
simultaneous affairs. Am I sick or normal?*

M: I've been on a lot of erotic trips. I rank them, now,
as I look back, on levels of comfort and gratification.
Marriage, which I'm currently on, gives me the greatest gratification that I've ever had and the greatest

comfort, though not necessarily in a day-to-day sense all the time. But I had a trip a number of years ago that was extraordinarily comfortable and very gratifying.

I'd been living in New York for seven unbroken years. I'd been working and I had an apartment and was fucking around; having affairs, living with people every now and then, and having one-night stands. This was what you did in New York when you were single, where you taste whatever you can and try to figure out what you want and what feels good.

Over a period of two to three years I had built up a stable (which has funny connotations, because if people were part of my stable, I was also part of their stable). Everybody had a little stable—stable as opposed to wobbly, rather than a horse stable. Or staple, perhaps, is a better word. These women became staples to me and I became a staple to them. There was a point where there were six women who I had known for anywhere from one to three years who I had real friendships with and real understandings with and a good erotic trip with. On any given night of the week I could open up my phone book and call any one of them interchangeably. Whichever one of them was available that night and wanted to see me, I would see, and go there and relate to her quite uniquely. Each of them knew that this was the arrangement, that she was one of many possibles that night, yet it was cool all around. It was just very nice. Friendship and eroticism entered a very easy blend. It was very easy, very lovely. No uppers or downers.

There were nights where nobody was home and there were nights where four people would call and everybody wanted to see you. So it had its own little difficulties. That went on for about a year or two and then went away. For a while I thought, "I want to keep doing that. That's the one I want to do because that was so nice," but I soon realized that I had cycled out of that one.

Having simultaneous affairs is extraordinarily difficult. On the one end is rampant loneliness and promiscuity. Coming out of your apartment every night, burning with loneliness and horniness. "I've got to get laid. I've got to find somebody." That kind of thing. Bad fucks where you wake up in the morning and wish you hadn't gone to bed with who you did the night before. Throwing people out of your apartment at three in the morning because you came and you couldn't stand them anymore. All those kinds of trips are in that.

Then there's the other end of the spectrum where you start getting into the commitment head . . . you start getting it on with somebody and it's suddenly, "She doesn't want you to have three others." And what do you do with that one? So to keep an intelligent promiscuity going is as difficult as keeping an intelligent marriage or an intelligent celibacy. It's a definite lifestyle which has its own difficulties, trials, tribulations, and efforts that you have to put in.

If you want to take that as a lifestyle, then you have to do it like you do everything else: consciously and intelligently. Be open and clean and realize that there are no guarantees. It might all disappear tomorrow, the same way that if you're married, your husband or your wife can run away, die, or divorce you. Now that was nine years ago. If I were that age today, in that same space in terms of my life and living in New York, I would probably be into threesomes. That was a very classical promiscuity. It was always me and Bette-Jane; me and Suzie. It never occured to me to get Bette-Jane and Suzie in the same bed. Today that would be more my style; like "I like you and I like her. The two of you met socially and like each other. Why don't we all do it together?" My hunch is that's where the promiscuity ambience is moving. Threesomes and foursomes. More affectionate inter-penetrations instead of being a little bee carrying the pollen all around—and gonorrhea along with it.

COMMUNES . . .

I had an interesting and fun experience on a commune in Eugene, Oregon, run by a drop-out mathematician; a brilliant guy who supported the commune largely by doing freelance computer work for the local IBM branch there. His trip was a very hip Tobacco Road. No doors were allowed on the bathrooms because his idea was that you've got to get to where you're not hung-up about having somebody watch you shit. That was just his ground rule. Another ground rule was that everyone had their own room with a door on it. That privacy you had to have. Then there was a communal bedroom where any night you wanted to party, there was always one going on. And absolutely no erotic restrictions whatsoever. Anybody fucked anybody else whenever they wanted. That was their only other rule. There was no such thing as "mine" and "yours," and it blew my mind. I was a little bit more uptight about erotic freedom than I am now (I am still very conservative in many ways despite my liberal activities) and I didn't know what to do with this.

I went there with a lady I had been living with for a while and it was suddenly, "Wow! There are fifty women here and I can fuck anyone who wants to fuck me." The women looked friendly. If you were a pleasant dude, sooner or later they would all get around to you. They had no prejudices. And I could have that. Paradise. The only trouble was that the lady I was living with was going to have to be doing the same thing. So I went through all of my changes about that.

The funny episode occurred as I was sitting on a log one day with about six or seven of these guys. They had been shoveling horseshit and some of them had straws in their mouths and they're rapping this heavy 60's psychedelic rap. This girl walks by who is about eleven years old and she looks like something out of an R. Crumb cartoon—the budding breasts, the budding buttocks, dimples, a smile of innocence, the clear bright eyes. Lolita on Tobacco Road. That look of recognition passed among the men which happens when the realize that they are all looking at the same woman and sheepishly smile at each other. A few winks and nods went around when this one guy slapped his thigh and said, "Almost ripe. Hope I'm the first one." I later found out that this man happened to be her father.

Their trip got to the point where it really no longer mattered. You want to talk about erotic freedom? Here it is. They were really living it out. Extraordinary. And it's still going. They've got about seven hundred to eight hundred people now. The only thing really wrong with it is that it's maintained by a very very heavy dope trip. A lot of acid is taken to keep it going, because if they don't keep it at that level, all of the inhibitions that they thought they had thrown out the window would come crashing in on their heads and the entire thing would blow up in their faces.

Q: I can see how a commune with fifty available sexual partners might be very nice. But don't you eventually come to miss not having any special feeling for someone?

M: Yes. The guy who founded it had two wives. He was legally married to one and then he and that one lived with another woman for several years until he began this commune. So they were his wives, but that didn't count for anything. The older wife had reached the point where in a given night she could drop acid, ball twelve men and six women on videotape (they had a videocamera that they would use) and watch herself on video, stoned, balling people while she was watching herself ball people, and she didn't know where she was going to get more.

You can take any trip to such an extreme that it kills you. And you can do that with the erotic trip. That was one of the dangers there. It became simply such a matter of sensation, that the checks that keep us from letting our sensations drive us into the ground weren't there very much. The other disappointment was the shallowness that you talk about. There wasn't that specialness.

THE EVOLUTIONARY ORGASM . . .

Q: What was your major moment of Metasexual consciousness? Of evolutionary thought?

M: I don't know if there was a "major" one, but I can tell you about one of the more dramatic moments.

I was hanging out with some of the original Anthos group—Julie and Joel and Irene. Julie and Joel were living on West Seventy-second Street and taking a lot of THC, which is a horse tranquilizer. It had an interesting effect on me. I sniffed some of the stuff and smoked some of the stuff and I found myself on all fours in their back yard gnawing at the base of a tree. So that kind of vibe was happening.

Then this guy and his old lady came over, who I never met before, and they were into a funny kind of swinging. They were married for twelve years and he just didn't want to be bothered anymore. He didn't stop loving his wife or seeing her as an erotic being, but he just didn't care. She got more and more uptight until he finally said to her, "Look. Fuck if you like. I don't care one way or the other." So she and I got into it.

There was a threesome going on. Irene and I and the guy were all rolling around on the floor. It was very weird with strange vibrations and beautiful moments, and then I went off into the next room. She came in and we wound up balling on a confessional chair, feeling like the Pope, balling this woman. And her cunt opened, just like a curtain parting. Suddenly the night sky and stars appeared. And my cock was like a spaceship going through the heavens. I couldn't see anything and I didn't know where I was. Then there was a very faint far off tingle, like a bell going off, way off in the distance, and I wondered, "What's that?" And I came back from that spot—from doing Star Trek—all the way back fifty-five million light years through the galaxies, through the sun—"Ah! There's the planets. There's the earth. There's the continents. There's New York City"—back into the apartment, back into the body, back to the *priedieu*, "Oh! I came!" So that was a very evolutionary orgasm.

5. THE PORNOGRAPHER

EROTIC WRITING . . .

Everybody who's not a virgin knows what fucking is. Whether you do it with a man or a woman or a dog, in twos, threes or fives, it doesn't matter. There is a vibration which takes place in the erotic realm, which translating it into something else, demeans it and destroys it. You need real poetry to talk about that sort of thing.

Q: How did you get into writing?

M: I was starving in the East Village in 1970, when I saw an ad in the *Village Voice,* "Wanted! Writers for adult novels." I wrote a chapter and sent it out and they wrote a note back saying, "It's too literary for the fuck market and it's got too much fucking in it for the literary market." So I brought it to a friend of mine who was an agent and he said, "Finish the book and let me see what I can do with it." I finished the book and he brought it to Olympia Press. They liked it, published it, I suddenly had a market, and I started writing novels.

The novels got reviews. *Screw* picked me up and I started writing for them and for *Gay.* Next, *Penthouse* and *Oui* were asking me to write for them and suddenly I realized that I had a reputation. But for three or four years I wasn't doing anything but trying to earn a living.

Someone asked earlier where you publish literary erotic novels. There's hardly anyplace anymore. Olympia's out of business and Grove is someplace else. The entire erotic trip in America has just vanished.

Q: What about Fear of Flying?

M: Fear of Flying is an extraordinary erotic book, but it's basically a literary novel. The eroticism is *of* the novel. Erotic literature is literature in which eroticism *is* the novel. It focuses on that. It also implies a certain degree of description; a certain hard core. And to find novels in which you have plot, character, literary quality, plus detailed and real and moving descriptions of fucking is a rarity.

Q: Can you name one?

M: High Thrust. Or *The Saline Solution,* if I can name one of my own. *Helen and Desire,* by Alexander Trucky, where there's an incredible scene in which a prim, prissy English lady is captured by Arabs. She is the quintessential type—higher than a Presbyterian school marm. The Arabs, of course, are grubby and dirty and vile and have twelve-inch cocks. And she has all sorts of adventures, like getting fucked on the steering wheel of an airplane while the airplane runs out of gas. It goes into this dive and she has an orgasm as the plane hits the ground—that kind of stuff.

But the scene where the Arabs have her: they take her to a room and they fatten her up. They feed her all types of sweet food. And the food has opium in it. Trucky used to be a junky, so he got into the whole opium head. And she just becomes this great, voluptuous mound of opiated flesh; so sensitive, that when breezes blow through the window and brush across her belly, she has rippling orgasms. Then, one night, six men come in a row, one after another, and fuck her until dawn, taking her on an eight-hour trip. That kind of eroticism: truly brilliant fantasy carried to its farthest level to where you can identify with what is inside of you.

Q: What is the best source of inspiration for your writing?

M: My problems. If I didn't have any problems I don't know that I'd write very much. Most of my writing has been an articulation of those things that I've had a lot of trouble understanding or coming to terms with. Many times I've stopped writing because in my Neapolitan superstitious head I thought, "I write about my problems. Therefore if I stop writing, my problems will go away." But it didn't work that way.

Q: Do you live all your experiences before you write them?

M: I wrote my first book when I was thirty-one or thirty-two. I had a lot of experience up to the writing of that. The first book was cast in the role of fantasy. It takes place in a fantastic Sex Therapy Institute and was called, *Mind Blower.* Everything that was in me at the time emerged in this form of fantasy. The book was a big success in its way. It never sold any appreciable amount, but people who are up on the genre said; "A bright new light has appeared. A great erotic writer," and all the rest of that flap. Maurice Girodias, who was publishing Olympia, said "You're the best since Henry Miller. Write us another book."

"But I don't know how to write a book," I answered.

"It was an accident." And it really was. It just came out. I think I wrote the first draft in two weeks.

The second book was *The Gentle Degenerates*, which was ninety percent autobiographical, and that was done by writing down whatever was going on. There was a work of fiction afterwards, but most of my books have been, "as I live them, I write it down," to the point of metaphysical embarrassment at times.

In the middle of *Gentle Degenerates* I was having a relationship with this girl who lived in California. I had met her out there and we got it on. Then I came back East and we were going back and forth and back and forth. A three-thousand-mile affair, which was really weird, and I was writing it down all the time. I was in the middle of the book and the middle of the affair and I called her one night. I'm talking to her and she asks, "I've really got to know what's happening and where you're at. What's the state of our relationship? What are you feeling? Where are you going? What's going down?" And spontaneously it just bubbled out of me: "I don't know. I haven't written the next chapter yet." She didn't talk to me for six months.

But for a long time, fact, fiction, who knows? It happens and you write it down. And then you write it down and it happens.

6. MARRIAGE

THE ACCIDENT . . .

I've told you about my first marriage. The second was an accident: the accident of pregnancy.

In 1968 I left San Francisco and went to Arizona. When I got to Tucson, I was sitting in a bookstore. A guy came up to me and asked, "What's your name?" I looked up, saw clouds passing through the sky, and so I said "Cloud." That became my name and it was very symbolic. I gave fantasy and relaxation classes in the open air and took people on a very very heavy psy-

81

chedelic trip. I had shaved my head and was walking around with a staff being a Zen Master.

One day, I was walking down the street and this girl came up on a motorcycle. She took me home, to the place where I was crashing, and we fucked. When I came, I remember her turning her head aside. I can recall precisely the look on her face and the way her neck moved. It made an impression on me but I didn't think more of it.

One thing and another happened and I never saw her again but when I moved back to San Francisco, she got in touch with me, and informed me she was pregnant. So I borrowed a car and went to see her with Kay—who was an old lover—and Shirley, who was the former lover of a friend of mine. First we stopped in San Francisco, then we stopped in Los Angeles to see Judy—who was another ex-girlfriend—and we drove down to Tucson, me and these three women.

We get to Tucson, back to old scenes; hash and grass and peyote and wine and the sun. This girl, Jane, was minding the dogs for a rich couple and also minding their place, which had a swimming pool. So there was swimming naked and all the rest. Jane tells me she wants to get married. I say I don't want to marry her. She insists she wants to give the child a name. She wants the child to have a legal father and if I marry her she's going to have a baby and be Mrs. Vassi and that would be all I would have to get involved with. So like a schmuck, I believe her.

We had three or four days of getting higher and

higher and higher. I visited her mother. She hasn't told her mother yet. I informed her that Jane was pregnant, that I didn't want to marry her, but was doing so to give the baby a name. And the mother says, "Jane has spent the last six months in an insane asylum and is not very stable." I didn't know what to do with that. I just said, "We're going to go to Nogales and we're going to get married and then I'm going to split."

We go there, all five of us. Shirley and Kay and Judy are my witnesses. It's one of those dumpy little rooms with an overhead fan going slowly around. It's conducted entirely in Spanish. Then I'm actually, physically, legally married. And my wife is pregnant.

We get in the car, go back to Tucson, have a really nice night—good fucking and good feelings and all of that. The next morning I wake up and my head is into, "Okay. I'm going to split. But how can I leave? I'd be running out on a wife and child." Two days went by where I came off the grass and the hash and the peyote and the getting married and being told I'm going to be a father and the sun and the swimming pool. And I decide that I really have to get out of there. Then it got ugly.

She cried and held on. I felt bad and suddenly wondered, "Maybe I really love her and it's destined by God." But I wrench myself away and head back to San Francisco. A month later she follows me to San Francisco, where again I tell her I don't want to be married to her. Yet this time we have a spiritual wedding. We get my friend Jim, who's into the occult, and

he performs a spiritual ceremony while I'm still saying, "This doesn't mean anything." Now I'm legally
and spiritually married and I'm going to have a baby
but I still don't want to be in this thing. I send her
away with much tears and more bad feelings and
more wrenching and that was the last contact I had
with her. Later, I heard she went to Los Angeles and
became a junky. I heard she went back to an insane
asylum. I heard she had an abortion. I heard she had
the child—all these stories and conflicting stories
through various grapevines. So I really don't know
what happened.

When Royce and I decided to get married this time,
I told her the story and she said, "Don't you think you
should find out whether we can get married or not?"
So I called Tucson, got Jane's aunt, who gets scared,
and gives me her brother. He gets scared and finally
gives me the mother's number. This is the woman I
talked to and spent an evening with; a strange relationship. I said, "Hey, I'm getting married again and
want to know if you folks ever had the marriage with
Jane annulled?"

I got twenty minutes of sheer blister. She just took
the skin off my soul. She called me all kinds of names
and let me know what a shit I was. After which I
accepted it all, said, "You're absolutely right. I can't
argue with that. But I want you to understand that I
had similar things happening to me. Whatever she
went through, I went through hell, too. I didn't skip
gaily away. If you want to read about it, it's in my
book. Get a copy of *The Stoned Apocalypse*. The whole

story's written including where my head is at, what I
was going through, and what happened afterwards."
That kind of mollified her. She said, "Okay. All I will
tell you is that you can get married. I won't give you
any details. I won't tell you that much because it's too
much satisfaction to give you. But you can get married."

That was my second marriage.

ROLLING A BIG ONE . . .

*Q: You're married now for a third time. What motivated
you? What does marriage provide for you? And how do you
expect, with your lustful background, to reign yourself in?*

M: When I got married I really didn't know the
person I was marrying. Royce and I had known one
another for nine months, but for a three-month period we didn't see one another. I was living with
another woman at the time, Royce was seeing two
other guys, so it wasn't nine solid months together.

Personalities aside—why this particular woman
rather than another—it seemed to me that if I could
take all of the trips I had been into and synthesize
them into a single life vehicle, that would be the most
masterful stroke I could take. That was the challenge.
I looked at marriage and understood all the aspects of

it that were negative, the traps, the things that could happen. I tested myself against them, decided that I was strong enough, had learned enough, could be consistent enough, and took a certain pride in rolling a big one; doing a very extreme, pure trip. Fidelity till death do us part.

Part of that was a religious thing; my religious trip of wanting to have the most righteous trip for me and the purity of having a unitary "I." The other part was a literary, social self which was already beginning to formulate how I could take nine books, my life, all that I had put together, and transmute it to what seems to be the exact opposite of everything I had seemed to be tending toward. I had reached the point where I said, "I have transcended bisexuality. I am capable at any time, with any person, of any kind of erotic trip whatsoever. I have mastered the eroticum. I can call forth instant passion, instant expertise, instant involvement; all of these things, like a master actor on the stage. Put me in an erotic situation and I can totally master it." Now given that, what I am choosing is this very high, pure, austere path. And I couldn't turn it down. I couldn't turn down that brilliant vision.

With it, of course, I had all kinds of misgivings. There was an echo, not quite as strong, but an echo of the first marriage. A lot of people saying, "Oh? You're getting married? Jesus Christ." General griping from people I didn't know that well who just had something against marriage. But people who knew me quite well said, "Hey. You're doing that thing again

that you've done over and over and over again and
that has caused so many people so much trouble.
You're a little older and a little wiser and your ra-
tionalization is a little more sophisticated, but you're
going through the loop once more. Why?"

I got defensive about it. Like when I fought the air
force and the world, I fought myself and I fought
Royce. Then I'd get carried away and tell myself
things that I very much wanted to be true in order to
carry out my intentions, so that I missed some of the
discrepancies between that shining vision and who I
really am and what I really need.

What's central now is, "Is it going to be possible for
me to attain a hollow, flexible emptiness—as the Zen
people say—which will integrate that vision that I had
into some kind of form that I'm really comfortable
with down to my roots—conceptually, emotionally,
and what have you—in order that this vehicle continue?" Can I be integrated in this?

Sometimes I can do this and it's no problem. When
I can't, I work on it internally, which is okay, and at
other times externally, which is messy, causes fights,
and goes on heavily at times, too

Will it work out? I just don't know.

I LIKE MARRIAGE . . .

I like marriage. Like anything else in life it has its rules; its dues to pay and its down and ups, but I feel congenial with it, even if it's a pain in the ass sometimes. Occasionally it gets in the way of the person that you're married to, where you don't see the other person but you see the "marriage." That's weird.

FIDELITY . . .

Q: Your view of "faithfulness" seems so different than mine. I don't quite understand what you mean by it.

M: Faithfulness used to mean something mystical to me. You were FAITHFUL. Faithfulness is nothing more complicated than an agreement. Two people decide that, everything considered, this is the best way for them to live their lives. They take all kinds of factors into consideration: jealousy, boredom, missed opportunities (for there'll always be somebody around that's turned on to you or that you're turned on to)—and you say, "All that being equal, the thing that I feel will make it best for me and best for us is that we live in such and such a way with each other."

You make that agreement, and then you work it out.

The definition of fidelity in my marriage is that we don't make it with anyone but each other. There are some people who can be faithful on different levels.

On the other hand, if my wife came to me and said, "I met another man and I dig him more than you and I want to be off with him," then we have to renegotiate. Then it becomes a different case. Then you simply say, "The agreement that we had has been called into question. Where are we? Do you want to stay married? Do you want to go work this out and see if you want to come back?" Or, on the basis of her telling me that, I say, "If that's the case I don't want to be in this marriage anymore." But it's an agreement. You agree to the ground rules of your relationship. It's almost like business. It's a contract with each other. Infidelity is nothing more than betraying your word.

If you fuck somebody and you come back and say, "I've fucked somebody," you haven't really been un- faithful. You've said, "I've done this and broken our compact," and then you leave it up to the other per- son to decide what they want to do in relation to your agreement. If you go off and fuck somebody and you don't tell, you get away with it if the other person doesn't find out, but you've been unfaithful. In old- fashioned terms, you've committed a sin. You've bro- ken your word. You've demeaned your own human- ity.

So fidelity consists of mutal respect, honesty and keeping a contract, whatever that contract is.

SHARING . . .

Before I was married I went out with some women, and while I didn't have any formal contracts with them, I knew that if I slept with someone else, they'd be hurt. I went about and did it anyway, told them about it, and they were hurt. That was a form of infidelity, but it wasn't technically so.

I've been married twice before. Once it was an aberration and lasted only five days. But when I was twenty-four I was married for a year and I was faithful for that year. When I found that I didn't want to be anymore, the marriage fell apart.

Royce (my wife) and I have talked about experimentation; things we'd like to do. One of the things I'd like to do is to go to bed with another woman in a threesome. But I don't want to have anything to do with the other woman. I want to see her and my old lady make it for several reasons. One is that I would like her to do that and I would experience just what that would be like. I would learn something from it. So we talk about that. It might happen, it might not. We're not stampeding into it. It's nothing we have to do. If it happens, it happens. If it doesn't we're not going to be lacking for anything.

There have been a couple of times I've had a fantasy of having another man in bed, where I've said, "I could really have another man doing you while I'm balling you. That really gets me off." But we both understand that if I took another man to bed, we'd all have to face my jealousy. So we're not about to do that till it's all cool. If it never gets cool, that'll never happen and that's okay.

There was one man who was a lover for awhile. I had many gay experiences but never had a love affair with a man. I'd had love affairs but no fucking. This was the first man where they came together. It was love and we were balling. It was a beautiful, beautiful thing. Then, at the end of ten days, we looked at each other and said, "You know, either we're going to get married or it's getting ridiculous."

"We can't get married," he said, "we're both men."

"You're right," I answered. "Why don't we just be friends." So we became very very deep friends.

Royce and I saw him this summer. We didn't ball, but we loved each other an awful lot. We realized that we could, at any time during the next twenty years, just have that love for each other and have it be physical. We talked about this a few nights ago and I said, "If there were any man in the world, it would be possible with, it would be him. I really feel you could go to bed with him and there wouldn't be anything of even the foggiest flap approaching the jealousy point. Because it would be a shared thing."

With most men, I would feel that somehow or other, they are cutting me out in order to get into my woman. Only one can fit in that place at one time. And if he's there, I'm not. "What is he doing there? Why aren't I there?" But if I can do that with a man I can make love to, then I know he's there as much for me as for her. Most men would tolerate me enough to ball her. Why do I have to bring someone to bed for that? But an equal sharing of three is a beautiful experience.

THE PARTY . . .

We know these people in Woodstock who've been married for about ten years. We got to know them pretty well, Royce and I, to a point that after a few drinks and a few joints, everybody is pretty straight and honest—in an oblique way—because this is an artist's and writer's circle.

One night this woman was getting into a whole erotic trip. We were doing a lot of smoking and drinking and dancing. Visions of orgies, like sugar plums, were dancing through my head. She's about ready to take on forty Hell's Angels. Her poor husband, who's had six joints and eight drinks and has been writing a book for the last four years, he'll fuck her if he really has to, but he's not into it just then. He's into an ex-Catholic writer's space. But she's for the Hell's Angels, and she's getting higher and higher and higher.

And I'm feeding her. I'm throwing little bits of meat to the piranhas, to get them excited. It's a party, right? Everybody has a good time in their own way. Finally, she says to her old man, "Do you realize I've never had another man but you for ten years? I wonder what it would be like?"

He rises, slowly, out of the depths of his deep funk and says, "Do you realize that it's as valid and as meaningful an experience not to have had more than one man for ten years than to have had a lot of men for ten years?"

It punctured the entire bubble. I was pissed off. It put a damp towel on the party. They were going to start showing dirty movies. But as always, the things that upset you most are the things that you learn the most from; such an obvious truth that got so lost in the hubbub of the erotic revolution—that fucking forty-two people a month is not better or worse. It's as real and valid a human experience to make it with only one person.

If you understand that, you should do that. If you're not into strict monogamy, you should do whatever it is you want to do. But for God's sake, don't keep shuttling back and forth between the two realities. Because you're just going to wear yourself out.

BRIEFINGS

OPENNESS . . .

Q: What makes you so comfortable talking about your personal life?

M: I honestly don't know. I'd always been secretive. Once I had a party and invited thirty or forty friends and realized that with each one of them I had a unique thing that none of the others knew about; forty parts of me spread out. Then, in 1966, during my introduction to the marijuana head, I suddenly viewed being stoned as a different way of life. I was living with a lady at the time and I had locked drawers and secret codes—like DaVinci—writings in my notebooks. One day it popped and I said, "I don't want to have secrets anymore." It just unlocked everything and threw it open.

Since then it's been more and more and more disclosure. The interesting thing is that the more I disclose, the more honest I have to be in my life. Because disclosure is only possible when you have nothing to hide. Since I'd done a lot of things I felt I had to hide, I had to get my head together in such a way that they didn't seem shameful to me anymore. That meant I had to find out what was beautiful and human in those acts.

WORRY . . .

Q: Do you worry about your reputation? About your career? Or that your forthrightness might get you in trouble?

M: Yes. Because sometimes we worry about things we're told to worry about but don't really need to. It's true of all of us and it's simple neurosis. You start being conditioned at an early age to worry about certain things. Then you ask yourself. "Should I be concerned about this?"

We're all to one degree or another worried about careers. Everybody wants to be a success. What if you really wound up a bum? Did you ever walk through the Bowery and see these guys? A lot of them are wrecks. They tried and they failed and they fell to the bottom. But you see a lot of them that are quite content. They get fed over on Third Street, winter comes and they go to Florida. I used to see a lot of them in California, where it's easier to be a bum because of the weather. Some of them have gone on for forty years; from Arizona to Oregon, as the seasons change. Odd jobs. If you ran out of work you spent several weeks in the insane asylum. Or jail.

I worked in an insane asylum for three months. I met one guy who was a professional patient. He'd been in and out of the insane asylum for years. He wasn't crazy. The therapist would come and say, "DANCE THERAPY!" And he'd mutter, "Shove it, sister." He didn't want to be bothered.

So we're all worried about things that we needn't be bothered by.

SHYNESS . . .

Q: *How about shyness. Are you still shy?*

M: I can't walk into a bar and pick up a girl. I don't know how to do it. If I got to the point where I was actually talking to a woman, I would probably say, "Do you want to fuck? I don't believe in being devious. I'll show you my books. I'm a great erotic genius, so I've got a right to ask, 'Do you want to fuck?' right off the bat. Actually I'm not being crude, I'm being very subtle." It's that type of shyness, for I don't know how to do that sort of thing.

My best introduction is when somebody introduces me. A friend comes up and says, "Here's Milly," and Milly and I talk in a very neutral situation for a while. Then I can sort of lie back, look at Milly out of a corner of my eye, see who she is and sense how she's seeing me. And if there's a little something happening I can talk to Milly a bit.

ONE LINERS . . .

Q: How can you tell if your son is a homosexual?

M: Ask him.

Q: Where can I get some good dope?

M: You're getting good dope.

Q: Do Marxists fuck?

M: Only on posters.

Q: How can we get love back into sex?

M: By fucking everybody you love.

NORMALITY . . .

Q: Are the Metasexual acts you describe more enjoyable than the normal acts?

M: The only abnormality I know of is damage. That's not human. But even scars aren't bad. If someone says, "I want a cut," as in the movie, *The Night Porter,* when you give that somebody a cut and it heals over, that's okay. The whole notion of "normal" and "perversion" is so weird.

We've been talking about piss drinking recently. It's been a recurrent topic around our home. At first it was very dirty. My trip was, "Having somebody piss in your mouth is the dirtiest thing you can do. How vile can you get?" And then you realize that children do it. Animals do it. In certain cultures urine is used as a medicinal substance, to treat skin rashes. Or it's used as shampoo. Or as a mouthwash. It's really sterile, unless the other person has a disease.

A few weeks ago I was with somebody, eating her, existing in that fantastic way in which I just souled into her body and she into mine. It was so tender and intimate. And I wanted something at that moment. I wanted urine; that warm, salty flow because it was from somebody that I was loving so much. It was extraordinarily erotic, vibrating with desire for that particular substance. You can make that abnormal if you want to. You can say, "Hey. This is really kinky."

Q: Does normal, then, have to do only with your own view and not anybody else's?

M: It depends on whether you're alone or with people. If you're with others you have to deal with consensual reality. You have to understand that you have two or more unique perceptions of reality in a given space. And you must find a consensual reality which at once allows everybody their unique perception and allows you all to communicate over a common wavelength.

If you come to my house, I don't want you to shit on the rug. I really don't. I don't consider that normal. If you do, I don't want you coming over to my house exercising your view of normality. It's as simple as that.

I hate to harken back to *Playboy* type cliches, but "consenting adults" does define normality. There's a catch, though, regarding the term "adult." Whether someone is truly adult is rarely a question of how old they are. If you really know who you are and you're with someone who really knows who he or she is, and you decide to do a thing, what can be wrong? As long as there is agreement, it could probably go up to and even include murder. If somebody says, "I actually want you to kill me." And if you say, "All right. I want to do that. I'll do it," it's a compact between two people. It has nothing to do with anybody else.

SEX CRIMES . . .

Q: How do you connect sex and crime? Where there is no consent? Or where people like Kalinger and his young son commit crimes, then sexually utilize and even murder their victims?

M: I've been tied up and at the mercy of somebody else. There was a surrender that took place that was very gratifying. I struggled and I fought, went through changes and told myself, "I don't know if I want it. Am I going to get hurt?" and all the rest. But when it finally became apparent to me that I would not be able to get out of these bonds, I just surrendered. For I could do nothing, and it was a strange sort of relief. A beautiful relaxation took place.

Luckily I was with someone who didn't want to kill me; who didn't want to damage me. The people who kill and damage are those who haven't made that distinction; who haven't stopped at saying, "Yes. It's nice to surrender. It's nice to render somebody helpless."

How many times have you been with somebody and said to yourself, "If I could just tie them up and fuck them. If they would just stop jumping around so much and getting so excited." So there's that impulse to simply calm it down. Those who tie others up and kill them have lost that perspective, lost their humanity, and don't know what they're doing.

Now there may be a type who gets conscious pleasure from rendering someone helpless and sticking a knife in them. If they exist, then all I can say is insofar as I'm human, I can appreciate the vibration of it. But unless it's a willing victim, it's a crime and should be stopped. That person should probably be impaled on a hook.

Q: Can you explain Kalinger bringing his thirteen-year-old son with him to rob and rape?

M: Misery loves company. Maybe he had a really perverse variation of the notion where every father wants his son to take over the family business: "My son. Someday all this will be yours!"

ANIMALS . . .

Q: Have you ever had sexual relations with an animal?

M: Only the human kind. I once tried it with a cat

when I was a kid. I was in my first Portnoy phase of masturbatory joy and was looking for things to stick it into besides my fist. I tried the cardboard roll of toilet paper and wet it, got shavings from the barber shop and glued it on the inside of the cardboard roll. It was still at the time when I thought that the opening of the cunt was a little bit below the belly-button.

Anyway, I found this cat in the alleyway, took it up to our apartment, and didn't quite know what to do with it. I sat it on my lap, began masturbating, and tried to do something with the animal. But I barely knew what to do with humans, much less a cat. And cats have that exquisite consciousness. This one looked over its shoulder, looked me straight in the eye, and its entire expression was, "Just what the fuck do you think you're doing?"

Q: Why have you never had an animal?

M: Why no animals for me? I tried the cat and the cat put me down. I've talked to guys who've grown up on farms, and they've told me that if you haven't fucked a sheep you're really missing out on one of the experiences in life. I would imagine that if I lived on a farm and there was a horny sheep there and I had an experienced guide who had done it and knew what it was about and knew how I could do it without getting my balls kicked off—or whatever you have to watch out for with sheep—and if he took me up to the sheep and said, "Hey, man. I want to introduce you to a treat," I think I'd probably fuck the sheep. I'd ask my old lady if she'd be jealous, and I think she'd probably be cool behind it. But it hasn't presented itself to me in any way where it could happen very easily. I'm a city kid. I've only lived with dogs, cats, and roaches.

There's a fine science fiction novel in which a space ship enters the solar system and starts eating up the moon as food. The creatures inside this thing are cats They have claws and cat faces, but they're intelligent and can speak and they can handle the controls. They capture a man from earth, who to them is just a monkey; an inferior form of life. And he falls in love with a cat.

Finally, out of pity, the cat lady allows him to ball her. He goes out of his mind with the sensuality and the writhing and the sounds and the purring and all the rest. The next morning, he gets up and she seems very cold to him. He asks, "But the joys and the beauty that we experienced last night?"

"I felt barely a thing," she answered.

"But . . . but . . ."

"Do you realize," she says, "that if I had let myself go you would have been torn to shreds?" And that gets us into the way cats fuck. The yowling that goes on. Two, three, four, five hours of incredible sounds.

Has anybody ever seen cats fuck? The male mounts the female who's all scrunched down. Her tail goes up, her hind quarters go down, and she does the tremendous tease. The male mounts her and grabs the back of her neck with his teeth. By the time they've finished, she has no fur on the back of her neck; he's chewed it off. There is clawing and scratching and sounds. When he comes and pulls out, he better be fast because her paw will whip around, ready to take a hunk out of him. She's pissed off because he took all the fur out of the back of her neck. There's another fine book called *Sex Energy*, by De-Rock, in which he explains the way snails fuck. Snails are hermaphroditic and they have their sex organs in their heads. When two snails get together one sticks his thing in the other one's slot and the other sticks a thing in the first one's slot—these things and slots being connected to their heads. Then they release these darts which are quite painful and sometimes cause death—the clear equivalent of whips and chains. So they have at each other with these darts and they thrash around with this pain going on and all this time they're doing a double fuck in their heads. You look at that and you think, "In relation to snails, how dare we consider ourselves erotic?"

As in most other things in the animal, fish and bird kingdom, it seems to me that the human species has traded in specialization for versatility. The dues we pay for our versatility is mediocrity. We're not really excellent at anything. We don't have any incredible act that matches the soaring of an eagle. Maybe some poetry. Maybe language is our thing. I'm not sure. Or music.

But you listen to whales sing and you think, "Jesus Christ. We're just monkeys with pretensions. We stumble around, always thinking we've found the riddle to the universe."

I've been into monkeys a lot. I've been reading

about them and I've caught three or four excellent documentaries on television about monkeys.

The monkey part of us is most comfortable in small tribal groups. Everybody knows everybody else. I'll pick the nits out of your hair and you'll pick the nits out of mine. We'll work it out and help each other stay alive.

I once saw a show on the way chimpanzees pass their day. They spend a couple of hours eating and grubbing for food, a couple of hours playing, a couple of hours grooming. They do a little fucking. And—this I really enjoyed—they spend an hour preparing their bed. An hour before bedtime they start looking for someplace to lie down. They get their leaves and things, figure out where they're going to rest, and then they sleep. They get up in the morning, scratch around, eat and play and fuck and groom and sleep.

I looked at that and I thought, "Western civilization is definitely a regression from that state."

PERFORMANCE . . .

Q: How do you deal with the need for sex and the fear of getting a poor performance rating.

M: Sex as Sex is that if you make a baby, you get an "A" rating. Metasexual performances are something else.

For years I was a performer. It really pleased me to give the lady or the gent orgasms and have them be impressed with what a virtuoso I was and how long I could stay, how high I could fly, and all the rest of that. About a year and a half ago I asked myself what seemed to be a very elementary question (which shows how long it takes to sometimes ask the right question): "What am I getting out of all of this?" It's a lot of strain and a lot of work and what am I? Some kind of missionary? So I want to spread the Gospel every time I fuck? I'm not having a good time. I'd prefer to just lie there and be done to.

Your question depends on what you mean by performance. If you mean coming too soon, what's "too soon?" If you come and you have a good time and a fantastic orgasm and you feel like rolling over and going to sleep and that pleases you, the only question is, "Can I get somebody to do it with me?" If you can, fine. Three-minute fucks and the two of you can live happily together for the rest of your life. Somehow, if it's over and you don't feel right—if you feel guilty or shitty and have a funny feeling in your stomach— these result from all kinds of internalized psychological and religious assumptions which you have to deal with in your own way.

The essential thing in performance is being with somebody who isn't interested in your image, namely *yourself.* The minute you stop being interested in your image, that's when you stop performing and that's when you stop worrying about it.

IMAGES . . .

Q: What about dealing with someone else's self and not their image?

M: To the degree that you're not interested in your image you stop being interested in other people's images. Then you can begin to see through people. When people start coming on to you, you can say, "There's a screen and this picture is being projected. But who's back there?"

The baths give you interesting examples of this, because people go there specifically for some kind of Metasex. They walk around either with just a towel on or naked, so you don't have the status clothes give. All you have are bodies. Still, you can see the images.

You pass down the hallway and you see a dude standing erect, muscles flexed, looking posed and disdainful. Written all over him is, "Anybody who doesn't want to suck my cock doesn't understand what real manhood is." He's just laying that out so heavily that you have to smile as you pass; "It's a nice movie, mister."

There's an aspect of Metasex I call the Theatrical Mode. And the Theatrical Mode is when you do that consciously—when you say, "Let's do theater." Let's put on our best costumes, whether it be actual clothes or psychic heads or emotional states, and have the images arise. Then you let the images dance. It doesn't have to be all that complex. A joint of good grass will get you there. You just get stoned and suddenly the picture show begins, and you let the images lead the bodies where they will.

ROLES . . .

Q: What are your views on male/female sex roles?

M: There is a book titled *The Left Hand of Darkness,* by Ursula LeGuin. She is a science fiction writer. An anthropologist lands on a world which has a most interesting erotic makeup. For twenty-seven days out of the month, people are neutral. They have no gender. And then they go into heat.

When they go into heat they can go either way. They can become male or female: If you're with someone, and you're both neutral, and you both go into heat at the same time, you play this hormone game in which male/female start balancing back and forth with each other.

As usual, science fiction is one step above pornography in terms of being acceptable as literature. And it is a very profound notion in terms of how we be. We walk around with a gender for a good deal of the time when we don't need to use it. If you're not actually involved in fucking, being male or female is largely incidental. That our society is bifurcated along

the male/female line is, of course, one of the rousing
cries of female lib and gay lib and a lot of political
movements. That is, why do we be men and women
when we're not engaged in the men/women business?

POWER . . .

*Q: Do you foresee an end to the patriarchy that exists now so
that women will finally overcome?*

M: I grew up in a matriarchy. My father spent forty
years trying to assert his will to live where he wanted
to live. He tried everything. He threatened. He ran
away from home. He cajoled. He was reasonable. He
had friends come in to convince my mother. But she
kept saying, "No." For forty years she was the domi-
nant voice and determined where we lived.

I ran into an interesting statistic the other night.
Women own 80 percent of the wealth in the United
States. Not the corporate wealth. The individual
wealth. So women have a weapon, but perhaps don't
know how to use it. The power is there.

The question is, how do you get power? One of my
big things these days is The Upper Hand at home. We
had the cops called one night arguing about The
Upper Hand. Both of us were saying, "There is no
Upper Hand . . . I don't want The Upper Hand . . .
You take The Upper Hand . . . I'll take The Upper

Hand." It's like a hot potato. We embarrassingly burn our fingers if we hold it too forcefully.

We all exist on this earth. We all come in the same way and we're all going to die. So on an existential level we are truly equal. Rockefeller gets born with fifty million dollars. Somebody gets born with a silver tongue. Some get born with very little. Then we start to group it. The workers and the bosses, the Russians and the Americans, the men and the women. In the erotic realm there are the bisexuals, the heterosexuals, the homosexuals, and all the rest. And as much energy as you invest in that kind of conceptualization, that's how much power it will have.

The truly radical act is to extricate yourself from that kind of perception. A lot of my politically involved friends accuse me of "Quietism." That's a historical bit where every time the bosses take over and the masses can't rise up, they go sit on their Zen pillows or they go home and fuck. But I have a sense that if everybody did suddenly become quiet, all this noise of civilization which is driving everyone crazy (this incredible din, including the erotic overstimulation that we all suffer from; "I only got laid seven times this week and I haven't been invited to an orgy. My God. What's wrong with me?"), that kind of thing would just stop. We'd all look about and say, "What a movie that was. What a picture show. Who were the people who were doing that?"

ASS FUCKING . . .

Q: Why don't most women enjoy anal fucking?

M: Every portion of the body is capable of pleasure and pain. The only thing to do is to find out how you want your body to experience sensation. If you're intense to the point of pain, you get into pain. The anal sphincter muscle is extraordinarily sensitive. The first six inches of the anal canal are composed of incredibly tender mucus membrane. The sensations of pleasure that are possible there make it a good ten times more pleasurable, at its best, than fucking. You can get ten times more out of your ass than out of your cock, without any question whatsoever. What you can get out of a cunt in relation to an ass I don't know, because a cunt I don't have. But I imagine a cunt must be ten times more sensitive than an asshole. So that may have something to do with it.

MASTURBATION . . .

Q: So you still enjoy good, slow jerk-offs in front of a woman? Even better, by a good sensitive woman?

M: Jerking off to climax in front of a woman is something that I had been very inhibited about for a long time. I got into it for the first time a couple of months ago and it was a very beautiful thing. It's something I had wanted to do for a long time, because masturbation is such an intimate activity. You be a way that you don't be when you're with somebody else. And if you can have that and share it with somebody it becomes very trippy.

I'll buy the "even better" by a good sensitive woman. If a good sensitive woman could jerk me off as well as I could do it myself, that would be extraordinary. But that would be a long, long study and take much time for a woman to be able to do that.

I've often wondered about woman's masturbation. If I'm fingering a woman, am I doing it right? Am I doing it the way she wants me to do it? You ask and you figure it out and you get sensitive and you do all kinds of things but somehow you wish you could be inside her body for a moment to really know what it is.

LETTING GO . . .

Q: How can we not be slaves to our cocks and cunts?

M: Why not be slaves to our cocks and cunts?

There's a very interesting question I'm personally dealing with these days. Why don't I fuck everybody? On a given night like this, I could probably fuck ninety-five percent of the people in this room without any trouble at all. Maybe one hundred percent, for I haven't found anybody who would really give me a hard time. That is to say, *I* could fuck. I'm not assuming they would necessarily want to fuck me.

What is fucking? You're with somebody. You're rapping. You're drinking a little bit, listening to music. You're at the office, at home, at a bar or wherever it is. You're talking about the president, your ex-wife, your Metasex life, or about all of these things. Suddenly, you look into each other's eyes and there's a certain flash between you. You realize that the two of you could very easily take off all your clothes and just nestle down together, rub up against one another and have a good time. You know how it's going to feel. It's going to feel warm and exciting and it's going to thrill you and you're just going to enjoy each other an awful lot.

That happens more or less all the time in our lives. It might happen once a week or ten times a day. It might not happen for a month, but it happens often enough so that we all know what it is. So when I say I can fuck anybody in the room, I'm not saying that I'm so irresistible that everyone will want to fuck me. That's not the point at all. I am saying that there's no one here I couldn't get into that space with if they wanted to share that moment. Anybody who wanted to hang out for a while to just see if we couldn't get into it, sure. It's the easiest thing in the world. It's so easy, I wonder why we have trouble with it.

I don't think most of us allow ourselves to be aware

of how polymorphously perverse we are. When that first comes on you, it can be a little scary. When you realize, "Wow. I can suck a cock and eat a cunt and kiss a lot of people. I can do that all the time." And it can make you very uptight, because you think, "What if I let go? What am I going to be prey to? What am I going to be open to?"

Well, the only thing you're going to be prey to is yourself, unless someone picks you up, ties you down, and throws you in the back of a truck, which is a very rare occurrence.

There was a period of about five or six years where I must have fucked a couple of hundred people. Everyone I met. I was running a therapy workshop at the time and people were coming in to therapy looking for something. I'd say, "I've got something to give you." But once you learn what your liberty is, you understand what freedom means. Liberty is, "I can do anything I want." But liberty's a low level. Freedom, as Frederick Engels pointed out, is the recognition of necessity. "What is necessary? Don't be fancy. Don't do extra."

The whole trouble with the world now is that we have a lot of shit that isn't necessary. We have more than we need. Erotically, too. There is an awful lot. But what, precisely, do we need? When that sense of responsibility comes in, or a sense of aesthetics—like, "What's the purest line? What's the cleanest line?"— you can get very erotic with people all the time yet get more and more discriminating.

CONFORMITY . . .

Q: Why are we such conformists—afraid to explore our erotic desires?

M: We are a funny kind of animal. It's very strange. There was a line I put down once that "perversion is the only freedom fascism allows." Fascism is one of those catch slogans which to me means Conformity, a loss of the senses, and a loss of vitality of life and connection with the earth; of what's real, and of life and death. We live a peculiar neurotic existence, so that a lot of our eroticism is simply that; a mask to keep us from realizing that we're not really being human, that we're not paying attention to human questions but are just hanging on by our fingernails.

Our erotic problem is that we've got to survive before we can fuck. When you're young and don't need to eat or sleep too much, you think, "Fuck survival. I'm just going to fuck." But then you reach thirty and you say, "If I don't survive, I'm not going to fuck very much longer. So your priorities shift a little bit.

Now the only viable economic unit for survival in our society is marriage. When the white folks—our ancestors—arrived here, the Indians, throughout their many tribes, had many different ways of doing it. Polygamy, polyandry, slavery, and all kinds of shit going on. That's what the tribes were. Each tribe did it differently so they went off and became a tribe.

Then the Europeans came with their Cartesian

logic and they said, "Everyone do it the same way." So the economic foundation of the society became marriage. That was the only way you were allowed to do it.

This is where the erotic revolution flounders. Erotically, we can be as variegated as we like. But if we want to survive, we've got to return to marriage, because that's the only unit we've got that society will allow to exist. So you have a threesome, or a group, or a commune marriage, and you find they ain't going to issue no license for that. Your neighbors aren't going to be too happy about it. Automatically you become defined as counter-culture. And you're not. You're just *different* culture. This is true fascism. You can't exist in the country unless you do it in the way that is approved. But approved by whom?

Fascism is conformity. Whether it's enforcement from above or, as in America, where it's not enforced as much as it is volunteered. We're a nation of volunteer conformists. Nobody has to put a Luger to our heads or open up gas chambers. We'll do it the way we're told because we're such nice people.

LOVE . . .

Q: How do you define love?

M: You're sitting down and you're ugly or you're

dopey or your mouth's hanging open and you've got a
foggy look in your eye. Your fly is unbuttoned and
you're belching and you're just really being at home.
If somebody looks at you and says, "Boy. I'd like to
fuck that. That really turns me on," then you've got
something approaching someone who loves you.
Then you've got somebody who isn't hung up on how
you've got to get it on in order for them to be interested.

A lot of our erotic trip is trying to figure out how
are we going to be the best to somebody who'll think
we're the best. How are we going to turn somebody
on and get them to take care of us? Too often, on the
morning after the party, you have a headache and
want to brush your teeth and this person doesn't
think you're the best anymore. And that's disappointment.

EROTICISM IS A SENSUAL ACTIVITY . . .

Q: What is the relationship between love and Metasex?

M: If you're having Metasex with someone you love,
that's one thing and it's really nice. If you're having
Metasex with someone you don't love, that's really
fine, too. You might be doing all kinds of things. Love
and Metasex needn't have anything to do with each

other. Most of the eroticism we involve ourselves in doesn't necessarily have to do with love. Compassion, liking, digging, disliking, are sufficient motivation. So are giving each other Reichian orgasms to get healthy; passing the time when there's nothing on TV, or getting high.

Eroticism (Metasex) is basically a sensual activity. It includes all the senses, including thought, which the Buddhists list as a sixth sense, and with the kinesthetic sense—the sense of balance and movement of the body—which is the seventh sense. We're so starved in so many of our senses, that sometimes the only way you can get to smell somebody's asshole is to fuck them. Maybe you don't want to fuck them, you just want to smell their asshole, which sounds like a very weird thing, but it isn't.

We don't look around as much as we could. Few people allow themselves to do crotch watching—to say, "Hey. Nice hanging you've got there. Congratulations, man." Or, "Gee that looks succulent." Nor do we go about smelling people—their hair, their scent.

Yet there's a doctor in New Jersey who diagnoses people on the basis of their shit. He doesn't just tell if you've got amoebic dysentary, but reads shit the way an astrologer reads your chart. He can tell about your mother and your childhood and where you were born and your neurosis. He looks not just for the poisons but the character of the shit. Shit, like everything else, has a character. You can tell a lot about somebody by looking at their ass. All my close friends and relationships have nice asses, come to think of it.

You can look at an ass and get a sense of, "Hey. That's a nice person." Why just look at their face or listen to their ideas? But we don't smell each other or taste each other.

One of the only two non-Italian kids in my neighborhood was Polish. When he was six years old, he was found in the street eating some horseshit. We had horses in those days, pulling the cart from which vegetables were peddled. Horseshit is like straw. It's very dry. It's not like eating human shit. And he was simply sitting on the street as kids will do, curious, and chewing on some horseshit. The little kids his age started calling him Torsten Horseshit. Well I knew him until we were both nineteen, when I left the neighborhood. And at nineteen years of age people were still calling him Torsten Horseshit. These things certainly discourage sensual curiosity.

When you put your finger inside somebody—in their ass or in their cunt or in their mouth—at first you think, "Wow. I'm doing it." But sometimes, after all of that dies down and you simply get into the tactile quality of it and feel what you're feeling, then it's, "Gee. That's a nice feeling." So touch, taste, feel, look, hear the quality of the other person's voice and think. If you do that with people and if the great God Eros feels in a good mood and decides to smile on you, you'll have a Metasexual encounter. What you then do with it is nobody's business but your own.

SWINGING . . .

Q: The people I've run into on the swinging scene seem really scared. They don't even look in your eyes and seem the conservative type. I wonder how that comes about?

M: You're married five years or ten years. You and your wife like each other and know you're going to be together for life, but your erotic life lacks something. Depending on your adventuresomeness and sophistication, you've tried vibrators and you've tried all the manuals. You've gone to dirty movies, used a Polaroid camera, have attended sexual awareness groups and all of that but it still isn't happening. So one night, one of you says, "Why don't we try the foursome?"

Now we do a lot of things in life where an idea appeals to us, we go into it, and suddenly it's much more than we expected it was going to be. You get two couples and they say, "Hey. That's simple. You ball her and I'll ball her and we can do it in the same room or we can go into separate bedrooms. Then we'll go home and that will be our erotic titillation for the week." So you keep it basically light. You're balling the lady but you don't want to get really into it. Because if you do, her old man might get jealous or your old lady is going to get jealous. This has happened to me, too.

My choice was to step back from that. It simply wasn't for me. I tried everything possible to eliminate that particular type of jealousy. But jealousy is an

organic, natural response for me. I know the conditioned aspects of it, but if I have love with a woman
and I'm really into her and she's into me, I simply
don't feel right about her being fucked by another
man. Now it can be negotiated. I'm sure if it actually
came to it, I could work it out, since I'm much more
sophisticated than I was. But why? It's like scotch. You
can acquire a taste for it, but you don't have to. And
I'm into doing as little as possible at this point in my
life; just what's necessary. That hasn't been necessary.
Let other people get into it.

Four-person marriages are a different story. Two
couples know each other over a period of time, they
live in separate apartments in the same building, or
nearby houses in the same suburb, and they're into
each other's refrigerator. They lend money, play
cards, go on trips together, and they're really very
tight and very close. One night the idea comes up that
they really dig each other's old ladies and old men and
would like to ball. But to make the step of saying,
"Why don't we have a permanent arrangement? All
four of us?" that becomes really serious.

If we truly want to find out about the four of us, we
must go into it with as much commitment as we go
into our own marriages. We say, "Us two and you two
are going to share. We'll move into the same house
and we'll live as four as we live as two." And that's
beginning to happen. There are a number of communes around the country where there are four-
person marriages. It's too soon to tell, but it looks very
stable, very good, and very solid.

My sense would be, be serious about it as a four-some. Don't play those diversion games. If you can't really have passion with somebody, why fuck? If you can't really get it on because you're afraid of some-one's jealousy, then you're just diddling around. I don't put it down if you want to do that, but if you're serious about it you might just bump up to a new level which could be very, very opening.

JEALOUSY AND CONVENTIONALITY . . .

Q: You've said that you're still conventional in spite of what you've gone through. Elaborate.

M: I don't want anybody to mess around with my sister. That kind of conventional.

Q: Do you have a sister?

M: No.
But I have a wife. And I don't want anybody to fuck around with my wife. I'll punch them in the nose. That's the feeling I have. A conditioning thing, again. I struggled with that particular one, especially during the erotic Aquarian Age, when suddenly, "There is no jealousy! If you're jealous, you're square." Well, I didn't want to be square, so I pretended I wasn't

jealous. I started going through all those trips, like having an old lady who said, "I don't want to ball anybody else," and I insisted, "You must. To prove that I'm not jealous," though I didn't put it quite that way.

She finally found a guy and she said, "All right. There's the guy who, if I wasn't with you, I would probably ball."

"All right," I told her, "ball him."

She took him home and did precisely that. I don't know if she had her Ultimate Orgasm, but she was obviously having a good time. I told her to do it, so she was doing it, and I sat around saying, "I'm not jealous. I'm not jealous at all. There's not a streak of jealousy in me."

After he left I made her miserable for four hours. Never got jealous, though. Just made her miserable. Then, the next morning, I woke up and I thought, "By God, I did it. I got through the thing and I made her miserable for four fours and my jaws hurt from my teeth being clenched, but I wasn't jealous. I can join the club."

Two nights later, we went to see *Rashomon*. That film concerns murder and rape. The story is told from four different viewpoints. You see one and then it's reshot from someone else's perspective. When the wife tells it, it's about going to the woods with her husband. This brutal bandit comes, throws her down, and violently, viciously rapes her. And, "Oh, God. That's terrible."

Then you see it from the husband's viewpoint. He's

tied to a tree, the bandit throws the woman down—as
in her version—mounts her and starts to ball her.
Then the camera goes to his back. You see her fist.
This great, rolling, brutal bandit and this frail little
woman. She's pounding without any effect on his
back. She's protesting. And he's fucking her and fucking her and fucking her. Her pounding becomes less
vehement. Then it stops. Finally, her hand opens up.
Then, very, very delicately, she caresses his shoulder
with one finger. This is what the husband sees.

We were at the Twelfth Street Cinema, on Twelfth
Street and Sixth Avenue. The folks were there who
used to go in those days, all watching *Rashomon*, this
great art film, and being transported by all the levels
and what a great genius Kurosawa is. And the minute
her finger brushes his shoulder, it suddenly dawned
on me—a light went on—and I turn around to her
and at the top of my lungs I shouted, "YOU CAME! I
SAW YOU. YOU CAME!" Everybody in the theater
gasped, jolted right out of whatever reverie they were
in in relation to the film.

I was jealous for a week. One week of pacing up
and down. "How could you?" and all the rest of this.
Her protestations to the simple reality that I prac-
tically forced her to do it fell on totally deaf ears. So a
couple of experiences like that and I said, "Hummm.
I'm jealous. I figured out something about myself. I
am a jealous person." Once I figured that out, then it
became simple. Whenever I got jealous I got jealous,
and didn't get hung up about it.

The way I see it today, people who dismiss jealousy

as an unnecessary emotion are talking Neo-Aquarian horseshit. It's a Tuesday night and it's rainy and I'm sick in my soul and I need my woman. I need her! I pick up the phone and I say, "Hey, woman . . ." And she says, "Sorry, Babes. There's another man here tonight," and she hangs up. I don't want that. If I have a woman, she's got to be mine. I don't mean I'd tell her what to do or that no one else can stick a cock in her every once in a while or anything like that. But she's got to be there when I need her.

Jealousy is pain. It's a danger signal. Now you can be neurotic about it. You can be picking up signals about a reality that's unreal, that doesn't exist. But it's a real signal. Your body is telling you something. When you get that gnawing in your belly, you've got to pay attention to what's happening there. To say, "Jealousy's bad. It's infantile. Let's not be jealous," denies part of your sensorium; the thing that allows you to perceive the world. It's denying an aspect of what you feel with. So the thing is not to get hung up on jealousy, not to be masochistic about it, but not to deny it. Instead, deal with it, feel it, and see what it's telling you.

I get shit for this view from my erotic peers. I received an invitation, recently, from the Bisexual Freedom League. They wanted me to do a fantasy workshop. I rap with that kind of person and the first thing they do is look askance. "Not only are you married but you're heterosexually married and you're faithful. And on top of that, you're jealous." It's like Trotsky and Stalin. I really feel like if I don't watch out, somebody from Bi-Lib may come by one day and drop an ice pick in my head for betraying the revolution. Luckily the revolution is very degenerate and laid back these days, so I don't have to worry about it too much. But that's the kind of feeling that you get.

The other thing about conventionality is that after going through all of the ramifications of my erotic trip, I found out that my basic drive comes down to, "every once in a while I get horny and I like to get laid." It's not more complicated than that. And I thought, "Is it that simple? Every once in a while you feel like fucking and you fuck? Can't it be more metaphysical than that?" So that's very conventional.

I find the things I do very conventional. Occasionally Royce and I will do a swinging from the chandeliers type number, but by and large I mostly enjoy the missionary position. It's nice. It feels good to me. And I don't give a damn that it's square or that the natives in Polynesia do it on trees. I like it and it feels good and my old lady likes it. We like doing it that way. I should be ashamed? It's that kind of conventionality.

When you find out what you like to do and then you do it, it's not square or hip. It's just who you are.

BONDING AND JEALOUSY . . .

Q: What causes jealousy?

M: Jealousy is usually a result of bonding. You're not jealous of anybody you're not bonded with. If you're the gay bachelor or the gay girl about town, you can fuck fifteen people in a month or a year or whatever your rate is, because you're not bonded. But whenever you're bonded with somebody (which I think is a Sexual, rather than a Metasexual phenomenon) something deeper happens than just fucking. When that bond takes place, you're in the jealousy realm. Something happens where you and the other person are in a situation—or on a level—where we can't be that free.

Now some people who are either very experienced or subtle or lucky, or what have you, seem to be working it out, whereby they can fuck at a level of intimacy, closeness and bondedness, and have that especially for them, and then fuck around outside; where you can ball somebody else, but "it doesn't mean a thing to me." However, even at that, sooner or later one of the partners meets somebody else who does mean something to them. Then the bond is threatened and you're back into the jealousy business again. So bonding seems to lead to the Jealousy and Possessiveness Syndrome, and it's just one of the dues you pay for that particular privilege.

Q: Do you think it's possible to have more than one relationship at a time?

M: In Nicolson's book, *Portrait of a Marriage*, he wrote of how his parents seemed to have worked out a very deep, lifetime, emotional person-to-person bond between them. They had homosexual relationships outside of that which didn't threaten that bond and that seemed to have worked fine. Maybe it was because it was a cross gender business. There's a lady that I've known who supposedly had a marriage like that. The husband's dead now, but they had that bond and both were free to have all kinds of other sexual things going. Maybe it's possible. Maybe two people can be so strongly wed in that sense that that kind of liberty occurs.

Q: Can you not bring deep bonding between you and more than one person within the same time-place area?

M: I've had brief flashes of that. Once, in San Francisco, I was living with a lady and having a very fantastic affair with another lady—Ellen, the one of the three-thousand-mile affair. I'd spend one night with one and one night with another. It reached the point where I realized it was a truly equal thing and that I felt deeply for both of them. So I did a fairly bold thing—especially for me at the time—where I took Kay, who was bisexual, over to see Ellen, who couldn't come.

Ellen never had an orgasm and the reason she started up with me was that I was conducting a relaxation class and she thought I knew something and I could make her come. When I took Kay over, the three of us went to bed. We kind of messed around a bit, and then I balled Ellen. I came but she still had not, and then Kay literally pushed me aside, with an attitude of, "Get out of the way, man. Let somebody who knows what's happening handle this." She proceeded to go down on Ellen and ate her for about half an hour. I was just sitting in the corner of the bed watching. I'd gotten over my tumescence, so I could be very Buddhistic in my detachment. And it was extraordinary.

Ellen came to the brink of orgasm fifteen times. Right at the edge. I kept thinking, "Kay's got her," when she'd skitter off. Again and again. Kay was the soul of passion and patience. She was also like a pro; one of those people who take pride in their work. She was going to do this thing and then it started to happen. The orgasmic cries began and you could hear a certain quality that let you know that she knew it was going to happen this time. She was going to let go and she was afraid and she was ecstatic and she was pissing and shitting and crying and it was all happening at once. It took about two minutes to build. The bed got at least up to Venus or Mars, far from the earth. "Oooaahhhh, Ooaaahh, Oooaahhhh!" It was an extraordinary thing. And then it was like a good pornographic novel—the rockets and the dams bursting and all the rest. Then it became a true three-way relationship.

It was good balling, not great. Kay never liked me all that much. She dug me in her way, but she never really respected me. She thought I was a lightweight. A kid. Not really serious. Ellen and Kay, though, now had a relationship.

Ellen had a boy, Django, who at that time was two years old. Kay and I moved in with Ellen, because she had a much nicer pad with a garden and more space. We lived together for three weeks. The first week we were just so ecstatic. "Wow! We've really done it. We've made three." The bond was equal and pure and clean and it worked because the triangle got supported. I think that split bonds fail so often because the other two ends of the triangle aren't happening with each other, so you're always going apart and the energy never gets fed back in.

We'd do things like getting up for breakfast, the four of us—San Francisco in '67 was very golden—and we'd sit around and think spiritual thoughts and bless our food and do that whole number, when it started to go sour. All of a sudden. Just like a twosome. I've been in twosomes that have gone sour but it was nothing compared to this. For as high as we got, that's how low we fell. When it's only the two of you, it's cool. You can just beat each other into exhaustion. It's not very nice or very pretty, but you know what's going on. Here, intrigue entered, where "me and Kay are cool. We know what's going on and we're hip.

What's the matter with you that you're sitting in a corner sulking?" Next, you're sitting there quite complacent when you notice a very subtle shift going on and there's Kay and Ellen together. They're cool and they know what's going on and you're sitting in the corner sulking.

It kept going around like that and got to the point where nobody knew who anybody could trust. Because we'd all betrayed each other so many times. Then one morning we got up and said, "What's the point?" So we split up.

SHOULD CHILDREN BE EXCLUDED? . . .

Q: Do you think that Django's exposure to these erotic comings and goings was proper?

M: I don't know. I've seen him subsequently and we have a very loving relationship. I saw him two years ago when I went to San Francisco to see Guru Vawa. I stopped in to visit Ellen. She was into Gurdjieff then and she was being very "observant." "Hi! Good to see you again after all these years," and all the rest, while she was observing my tone of voice and observing my posture. But Django was fine.

She and I were in bed one day. We were fucking and he woke up and crawled out of wherever he was sleeping and got into bed before we noticed. She freaked. "My God. Here I am being fucked and my son! All the books say that's the worst possible thing that can happen."

I was loose enough at the time (that is to say, I didn't have enough invested—sometimes shallowness pays off and you can do the right thing because you're not hung up worrying about it) and I just said, "It's okay. Let him join us." He looked around curiously, trying to figure out what was going on, and finally decided that whatever it was that was happening didn't interest him all that much. So he crawled up and lay next to her, put his head on her shoulder, sucked on her nipple a bit, and just went off to sleep.

My wife and I were talking about this two weeks ago and she said, "What do you think about that? Kids and sex?" I said, "I really think if a man and a woman are making love, that's probably one of the nicest things that a child can see." It gets back to the Lenny Bruce bit about the movies, where it's okay to take them to see *Psycho,* where a lady gets stabbed with a knife, but you can't take them to the porn flick where these two people are loving each other.

WHAT DO CHILDREN KNOW? . . .

Q: Do you think the child knew what you were doing? Or that he was ready for such an experience?

M: I knew a guru many years ago, a very wise old man who is still alive at one hundred and thirty. He knew an awful lot. I asked him one time about eroticism. He said, "What do you know now that you didn't know as an infant?"

"What do you mean?" I asked.

"Didn't you . . ." and he pursed his lips and made a sucking sound.

And what do we do, as adults, that is any different from that strong, central reaching out?

EROS AND ENLIGHTENMENT . . .

Q: It seems as though a lot of your search for yourself has been through your sexuality . . .

M: Metasexuality . . .

Q: And I wondered if you still felt that was a valid trip.

M: Oh, I've taken other trips. Dope trips. So called Spiritual trips—the Zen trip, the Gurdjieff trip, the Yoga trip. I've taken the literature trip, moving through words and poetry. The old Taoist saying is that "There are as many paths as there are human beings. Each person is his or her own path." Because we are all human, we share certain similarities in terms of our trips.

Q: What is Gurdjieff?

M: Gurdjieff was a bald-headed crank who died about twenty years ago; a Turk who caused more mischief in his lifetime than Jesus, Buddha and Mohammed put together. A very heavy man, ponderous in his consciousness. Very macho existential. Any day in which you didn't feel eighteen hours of continual terror was considered copping out—that kind of thing.

He said, "We say 'I,' as though, somehow, there were a unitary creature here. And we forget that the person who goes to sleep the night before isn't the same person who wakes up the next morning." You've fallen asleep and you're stoned and you've just balled and you're in love and it's beautiful. You wake up in the morning and you're riddled with hate. So who's this unitary being that can be so radically changed by a night's sleep?

For most of us, the Master's away. The Master's not home and all of the servants have the run of the house. When somebody comes to the house, the answer they get depends on which servant happens to be answering the door at any given time. You get a sexy servant or a surly servant, depending on who opens the door. That's who they meet and this is "I." The notion is to crystalize a unitary I, one who does not change, who keeps the same viewpoint always. That does not mean you don't go through changes. But your attitude, your viewpoint, your posture— your literal posture—is always the same. It gets into the Zen trip. The Zen people say, "Sit. If you can't sit, stand! You don't have to worry about your state of mind. That is your state of mind." So the notion is to fix your attitude and then you can go through life with some sort of direction and scope on what's happening to you.

Bhagwan Rajneesh says, "Most of us who talk about giving up the ego are like paupers talking about giving up their wealth." In the sixties, there was a lot of bold talk about giving up the ego, when you don't really have much of an ego to give up yet. For most of us have not developed a real ego, an "I" that doesn't change. He talks about Zen as being the ultimate ego-trip; Zen being the full crystalization of the ego. Then we have something to give up.

Q: You're talking about fucking and you're talking about enlightenment. Are they ever connected?

M: Fucking is one of the best meditations you can do, providing you pay attention. Gurdjieff said that the sex center is the fifth center, above the first four; the instinctive, the moving, the intellectual, and the emotional. Then there's the sex center before you get to the two really high ones. And if you can integrate at the level of the sex center, everything else falls into place: your thinking, your breathing, your emoting, and your moving. All of these things cool out. So if you can get it straight while you're fucking, that's probably one of the best meditations you can do.

Rajneesh, again, says that the only thing you have

to worry about while you're fucking is, "Is your breath deep and regular?" When I first heard that it seemed like an odd question. Then I became aware of fucking in relation to breathing, and I found that fucking was almost always equated with shallow hyperventilation or a holding of the breath, and then an explosion—"I'm coming! I'm coming!" When I began to see if I could come off that, all kinds of things began to fall away. Like violence. There's an awful lot of violence in fucking—not where you want to hurt somebody but a lot of driving and pushing. As those things begin to fall away and your breathing begins to get deeper, you find you have an energy which has nothing to do with jitteriness, but something that is very slow, very deep, very relaxed, and extraordinarily powerful for all of that.

Q: You're saying then that fucking can lead to knowledge.

M: Fucking can lead you to many things. It can be a bummer sometimes. You can be feeling really good and afterwards you're not feeling so good anymore. It can also lead you to a state where you're feeling really charged. Your energy's a bit low and you don't know what you want to do. Your woman comes up to you, pulls you off into a corner, and suddenly the juice is flowing again. You wonder, "How did I get off that?" for you're alive.

It can lead you to knowledge. Metasex is also a metaphor. Everything that happens in bed happens outside of bed, and vice versa. The more we understand that, the more being in bed stops being something so alienated from everything else. We really make funny distinctions.

Knowledge, ultimately, means perspective. There's knowing something and then knowing it. Another Taoist saying is that "you have to not know that you know anymore." That's the hardest part. Because you can get real, real smart. If you get stoned or high on a spring morning, or you're fucking or in love—whatever it is that does it for you—it's, "Ah! I know! There it is." But it's a bubble. It bursts. And when the bubble bursts, you're right back where you were with your habit and your weaknesses and your fears and your loneliness and your lies and your stupidities and all the rest of it, stumbling through life and not really knowing what the fuck is going on.

So you study and you learn and you work and you think and you ask and you talk and you figure out and you search and you search and you search. And you try to understand what it is. You can get so knowledgeable and so high that there comes a point at which you have to drop that, too. You've got to drop it because you're still fumbling around. You've got to take all of that and make it part of you. Yet you don't want to come down from that high awareness.

That's what happened in the sixties, when the whole psychedelic thing went kaplooie. Millions of people were into "I don't want to be disturbed. I'm understanding the universe. I am God. God and I are one." Meanwhile, the reality is grinding on. And you have to come back into your defects, into your hu-

manity, into your death, into all the weaknesses that
make us what we are. The whole erotic trip which had
been so ballyhooed and is now making a bit of a
revival here and there, is as real as physics or anything else. But it's not, by itself, going to save us. For
that we need a more centered point of view.

LIFE IS PAIN . . .

*Q: You said that Gurdjieff tried to teach a unitary "I."
Supposing that you're the type of person who likes to vacil-
late, who likes surprises, who accepts the fact that different
servants open the door all the time.*

M: That's a nice way to be. But it has its dues to pay
just like any other trip. There is no way of being that
doesn't have dues. Maturity consists of understanding
that fact. There is something about the nature of the
universe which says you've got to pay for everything
you get. There's no such thing as a free lunch.

Q: Who says?

M: I say. Pain and fear are inevitable with every
choice and throughout existence.

*Q: But are you distinguishing between primary and second-
ary pain?*

M: Life is pain! Life is suffering! Life is struggle! Life is strife! For everybody. What you're afraid of is only of interest to you. What I'm afraid of is only of interest to me. But fear is a universal. We all know fear. So why should we fuck around with differences? It's so insane. We can speak on a level in which we have a common language for all life; not just people, but dogs and cats and roaches.

I had an exterminator in a month ago, because the roaches were in the bed, and in the drawers, and hopping on people's shoulders. I pleaded with them and I pleaded with them. I said, "For God's sake, get behind the sink and you'll be left alone." But there was no communication, so the exterminator came in.

He brought the poison gas and the deadly chemicals were placed over everything. Royce and I came back the next day to find dead roaches all over. For weeks afterwards they'd crawl out, gasp, fall over and die. And I said, "Vietnam! It's no fucking difference. I ordered my air force to come and kill." No one can tell me that a roach likes to die any more than any of us do. They don't like it either. We're all one thing.

So if you don't understand that pain is a central fact of life, you're missing the point. Forget distinctions of "Is it primary or secondary?" When Buddha had his enlightenment after sitting under the tree, he said, "Wow. Once and for all I've understood it." The people said, "Far out! Man, you've got that two-foot aura around your head and you're floating eight inches off the ground and you've got that beatific smile on your face and you look so happy and chubby. What is it? Tell us the answer!" And he said, "Existence is pain."

Q: And everybody went away?

M: No. Thousands came. People are still coming. Billions of people have come over the last 2,500 years to hear that message.

And Jesus? The culmination. Where does it all end? "Nails through my hands?"

So once you understand that, once you see that this is a rule of life—there is no life without pain—then you can begin to do something about the pain. But as long as you try to pretend it's not real, that it doesn't exist, that it shouldn't be—utopian dreams of a land where nobody ever hurts—then you're not going to accomplish anything.

THE ULTIMATE ORGASM . . .

Q: What is the ultimate orgasm? Is it obtainable?

M: A few weeks ago I was with some friends. Three of the guys were gay, there was me, and there was a lady. We got to talking about things and she started talking about her childbirth—she had two children.

"You know," she said, "when I had that baby it wasn't under anesthesia, and the things I felt—the convulsions, the opening, all of it—was more than I ever felt in an orgasm that came from fucking somebody. That's the ultimate orgasm for me, having a baby." So that's one answer.

For me, I think, the ultimate orgasm is probably death. It's the final letting go. It's like, "All this practice all this practice all this practice and now the big one's coming. Can you do it?"

THE FUTURE OF CIVILIZATION . . .

Q: Do you think our civilization has a future?

M: If, by civilization, you mean the guiding mythos— the religion, the sense of movement, the sense of purpose, the sense of identity, the paradigm, the model, the philosophy—it's been dead since 1914. In 1914, all the things that we thought made us civilized, ended. The war in Europe, and then the second World War, proved to us conclusively that we are not civilized.

A lot of people are beginning to wake up and say, "Now wait. All the things that we were taught—Catholicism, Judaism, Buddhism, Mohammedanism, the Flag, the Buck, Momma, Poppa, Freud, Reich—

have not prevented World War I, World War II, the Korean War, the Vietnam War, the pollution of the planet, starvation, overpopulation, confusion and neurosis and psychosis in our daily lives. If none of these things have prevented this incredible horror that our world has become, then what do we look to? That's how you define the end of a civilization; when people in that civilization wake up and say, "How do we redefine ourselves?"

Western civilization is not dying because of the Vietnam atrocity, but because people in our civilization have understood that the myths which sustain them as a society are bankrupt. It's not that Catholicism, or Protestantism, or Capitalism is any worse or any better than Feudalism or Communism or anything else, but that increasingly people are waking up and realizing that these ideas that we have lived by are bankrupt. They are not worth shit.

Q: That does not mean civilization has to end.

M: Civilization as survival should not end. You should be able to pay a dollar and have the man realize what that dollar means. Unfortunately, as the conceptual aspect of civilization gets weaker, the survival aspect of civilization begins to fall apart. This is a revolutionary bind. This is the bind that every radical is in, and I consider myself a radical. That is, if you undermine the corruption in the civilization, what you do is begin to tear apart the survival mechanism. And you don't want to starve.

If a fire breaks out, you want the fire company to get there. If somebody's mugging you, you want a policeman on the corner. You want the mechanism of civilization but you don't want the mythic aspect of it which is corrupt and rotten.

Capitalism as a concept is shit. Catholicism as a concept is shit. Nobody believes in these things anymore. So everybody's saying, "How can we change our sense of who we are without interrupting the fact that the milk is going to come from New Jersey in the morning?" And everybody's walking a tightrope. We all want to change the civilization, but at the same time we don't want to die in the process.

The sixties ended with everybody saying, "Hey, man. That's the choice. We may rip it down but in the process we've got to make sure that the thing has some continuity. And I think there's been an unconscious agreement throughout the country to sort of keep it cool and keep the balance and see if we can work it out somehow so it doesn't come crashing about our heads, because we don't want that.

But as far as the contemporary scene is concerned, we are a long way from a tenth-century peasant in France who had the farm, and the feudal lord, and there on the hill was the cathedral which pointed straight to God. That's all he knew. We know. We know a lot more. We know we live on one of many multiple universes. We have television. We have LSD. We have cosmic consciousness. And massively. Not just an occasional saint or wiseman. Millions and millions and millions of people have awakened to an incredible level of consciousness.

What do we do? That is what each of us is here to find out. Each of us has our own private fantasy about how we're going to lead the people into the promised land, I'm sure. I won't lay my fantasies upon you about how I intend to lead us there.

Q: Won't progress help?

M: Progress is a myth. If you think that we, living in New York City, are at a higher level of civilization than the Indians who lived here before us, that is your primary myth. We really think we are living better than the Indians, the Egyptians, the ancient Chinese, the Romans, and the natives in New Guinea. We really fucking think we're better. And we're not. The only thing we have is that we've used some small segment of our brain to create a technology with which we are now destroying the earth. And by this we define ourselves as better? If anything, we're worse.

I was in the art room the other day and we were looking at pictures of naked women, and there were all these other women walking around. *Penthouse* magazine makes seven million dollars a month on sales alone, not counting advertising, simply because they were the first to show pubic hair. Our publisher considers that progress. A multimillion dollar empire based upon being able to see pubic hair. Just where are we at?

Q: Isn't this anti-intellectual? How can you just dismiss the values of our civilization? Aren't we better off than cultures which have mass starvation?

M: No. The denial of technology is not my point. The denial of the myth of technology is the point.

Q: We tend to measure things in terms of material progress rather than in terms of quality of progress.

M: Right. Let's measure it by some real measure, like the orgy. Do we really have better orgies today than they had in ancient Rome? Absolutely not. If anything, they're not as good. So if the quality of the orgy has gone down in over two thousand years, what's the value of our civilization?

THE FUTURE OF METASEX . . .

Q: Does Sex have a future? If not, why not?

M: Sex as opposed to Metasex comes down to are we going to survive the twentieth century? This is what everybody's really worried about. A lot of the fucking we do is done to avoid paying attention to the situation we're in, so we do a bit of aversion fucking.

Do we have a future as a species? Who knows. We

can blow it up tomorrow. We might poison ourselves in thirty years. There's no way to tell at this point.

Assuming we exist as a species, does Metasex have a future? Yes. If you consider that even celibacy is a form of Metasex, as I do.

The erotic ambience, the erotic communication, the erotic mood is the source of beauty and art. Our painting, our dancing, our poetry, our film making—and in my head, even our state of consciousness—are all variations of that feeling. And that feeling is nothing more than the healthy body in its full sensitivity, vibrating to the fact of being alive. That's what real eroticism is, sharing that vibration with somebody.

I would say that if we're going to survive, the more Metasexual we can get, the better our chances are. The trouble is, the minute you start getting at all sexy with somebody, you're immediately faced with some kind of choice. "Do I fuck? Don't I fuck? If I fuck, do I like? Don't I like? Do I get married? What does it mean? What does it involve?" It's getting so that you can't put your hand on somebody's ass anymore and just say, "Gee that feels nice."

EPILOGUE

By Richard Curtis

For Marco

To demonstrate the extraordinary effect you had on
  me
I would like to say this:
Every time I set out to write a tribute to you
It came out a poem.
I don't write poetry.
But that's the effect you had on me.
And here's my poem.

As you lay dying
I sat beside you on your bed and took your hand.
Intubated as you were, you could not speak.
So you expressed yourself with eyes whose quiet
   calm belied your pain.
And with a smile that reassured me even as I was
   groping for words to reassure you.
Most of all, you expressed yourself with the hand I
   held in mine.
You squeezed and I felt what was in your heart.
Then you did the oddest thing.
You scratched my palm with your finger.
I looked at you with surprise.
When I was a schoolboy, that's what someone did
   when he was coming on to somebody.
Surely that is not what Marco means given these
   dreadful circumstances! I said to myself.
But I came away from that last visit with my palm
   tingling.
And so you left me with a mystery to contemplate.
I don't understand it now and I don't think I ever
   will.
But that was you, Marco. You loved a mystery and
   you were a mystery.
People were mysteries to you, and the way you
   penetrated their mystery was to love them.
You loved them so hard, almost desperately,
As if you had to get to the center of them or you
   would perish.
Of course there is no center of anybody, people are
   too complex.

But we loved you for trying, and that's why you kept
  us all as friends long after the loving was over.
To come on to somebody as you lie on your deathbed
  battling for every breath is plainly preposterous.
But no one had a keener sense of the preposterous
  than you.
So here I stand, palm still atingle from your scratch
And I will wonder forever what you were trying to
  say to me.
What the hell were you trying to say?

Richard Curtis

---

*Richard Curtis was Marco Vassi's friend and literary agent